What people are saying

"David Russell really understands people...and business! His latest book, **Success with People** is designed to help you bring out the best in your employees...in a stress-free, natural way! Russell's **Success with People** is a complete, simple system for finding, hiring, and managing the people that are building and managing your company. Anybody that has employees should not only read this book...but keep it on their desktop for quick and easy reference. I love the straightforward, non-academic language David uses throughout this book. This is a must read!"

Jim Horan, President, The One Page Business Plan Co.
Berkeley, CA www.onepagebusinessplan.com

"*Success with People* is a must read for managers at all levels. David has captured the real key to success is surrounding yourself with successful people and helping them reach their full potential. In less than three hours you can learn the basic tools to managing people more effectively."

Steve Harper, President, Network Management Group, Inc.
Hutchinson, KS www.nmgi.com

"Based upon my 25 year professional career in Human Resources ranging from Fortune 50 companies to small start-ups, and being asked to teach at the college level, it is abundantly clear that any organization leveraging the power of the *Success with People* system can harness the collective energy of its people in a directed manner to propel the organization to achieve its goals. Having known and been with Dave at a start-up, I recommend combining this system along with a strong motivational management style and organizational culture to create a winning combination."

Tim Hansel, SPHR, Santa Rosa, CA

about Success With People

"Management books often provide a wealth of ideas, but few offer useful information about how to implement the good ones; Russell does both in *Success With People*. HR professionals should recommend this book to managers who want to easily learn a proven, effective system for managing people and to better understand the objectives HR is driving."

> *Johnny C. Taylor, Jr., J.D., SPHR*
> *Chairman*
> *Society for Human Resource Management*

"David has successfully captured the critical factors of motivating and managing employees to work as a team towards unified goals. *Success With People* will enable you, as it has enabled me, to quickly implement organization changing behavior that will positively affect your company's productivity and improve the balance in your employee's lives."

> *Chris Ellerman, Vice President – Professional Services*
> *Meridian IT Solutions www.meridianITsolutions.com*

"In the 1980s Tom Peters wrote about management by walking about - Russell has written the blueprint of how to do this in the 21st century."

> *Don Oliver, Vice President, Financial Management Services*

"This is a great tool for someone starting a business. Since I have 20 years of experience, I found *Success With People* to include several valuable reminders for me to help our business grow to the next level."

> *Mark Jacobson, President*
> *NetGain Technologies www.NetGainKY.com*

David Russell

Barnabas Smyth Publishing

Please note that much of this publication is based on personal experience and anecdotal evidence. Although the author and publisher have made every reasonable attempt to achieve complete accuracy of the content in this Book, they assume no responsibility for errors or omissions. Also, you should use this information as you see fit, and at your own risk. Your particular situation may not be exactly suited to the examples illustrated here; in fact, it's likely that they won't be the same, and you should adjust your use of the information and recommendations accordingly.

Any trademarks, service marks, product names or named features are assumed to be the property of their respective owners, and are used only for reference. There is no implied endorsement if we use one of these terms.

Printed in the United States of America
First Printing: August 2005.
Second Printing / Version 1.1 (December 2006)

Cover design by Bill Chiaravalle of www.BrandNavigation.com.

Library of Congress Copyright Registration # TXu1-260-991
Writers Guild of America Intellectual Property Registry: 1149754
ISBN: 978-0-9771659-2-6

Success With People and *TARGET Goals* are pending trademarks of Success With People, Inc.

DISCLAIMER: The contents of this publication, the book Success With People, and/or on www.SuccessWithPeople.com are intended for general information purposes only. Information contained in this document is not intended to be a substitute for legal advice or to provide legal guidance of any kind whatsoever. If legal advice or other expert assistance is required, the services of a competent professional should be sought.

Get a Coach or Join our Club

Consider working with a good executive coach. Friends won't hold you accountable and co-workers may not have the perspective you need to determine the best decision.

Success With People, Inc. has qualified coaches available. A knowledgeable and/or professional coach is one of the best ways to accelerate success and keep you on track.

A good coach helps you learn how to think more effectively on your own, provide inspirational insights and hold yourself accountable to manage others more consistently.

Visit www.SuccessWithPeople.com for more information.

Or join the Success With People Club

For less than $25 a month you receive the following benefits.

Monthly Leadership Coaching CD delivered to your mailbox

- 12 coaching sessions, each one based on a *Desired Result* of the *Success With People* system

- Additional content in response to Member requests

- Articles, documents, exercises, audio and/or video content to help your team develop as leaders

Members-Only Club Website

- Ability to ask virtually any question about how to manage talent more effectively – answers are given within 2 business days FREE   *(legal advice is NOT provided)*

- Access to the growing library of these answers

- Additional resources to help you develop a more fulfilling and productive work environment

Visit www.SuccessWithPeople.com for more information.

Thanks!

I dedicate this book to the following people who have encouraged and supported me through the tough times.

Terry, my wonderful, beautiful wife of 29 years

Our children – Jenny, Jeff (Nicole, his wife, and Annabella, our granddaughter), Luke and Arie

Mom, Dad, Phil, Janet, Grandpa and Buddie

Richurd Somers, John Rauschkolb Jr., Joe Everly, Randy Ferguson, T.C. Michalak, and Jack Hagler

A special thanks to the following people who read early drafts and provided suggestions for improvement and encouragement:

Jim Horan, President, The One Page Business Plan Co. Berkeley, CA www.onepagebusinessplan.com

Timothy (T.C.) Michalak

Janet Russell, Real Estate Broker, Santa Cruz, California www.beachouse.us

Gail Derreberry; Jim Finkelstein, www.FutureSense.com, Tim Hansel; Steve Harper (www.NMGI.com), Mark Jacobson www.NetGainKY.com, Mike Kulwiec (www.DentalMasters.com), Don Oliver, and David Stelzl (www.stelzl.us).

Refer a Friend

If you enjoy this book, please recommend it to others. Refer them to our web site (www.SuccessWithPeople.com) for additional information, our free newsletter and free sample documents.

Contents

Foreword

Too many people are disappointed to realize that they must manage people to succeed in business. The reality of starting a company or being a manager is very different than what they imagined.

Did you know recent studies indicate 80% of employees are so unhappy at work that they are actively seeking work elsewhere?[1] Losing employees costs tens of thousands of dollars and managing unhappy employees is a miserable job.

There is a better way. Retain employees by managing better.

In the past, I did not manage people very well. Then I took the time to dedicate myself to the following:

- ❑ Study the best practices in people management.
- ❑ Work for KnowledgePoint, a leader in workforce management software at the time and studied competitors with an open mind.
- ❑ Learn from seasoned consultants who taught the best ways to achieve objectives through people.
- ❑ Read, attended seminars, debated best practices, and devoured case studies.
- ❑ Test what I learned.

The *Success With People* system is the result.

Occasionally this book mentions a spiritual perspective because your faith (whatever it may be) directly impacts how you manage others. My local faith community (www.questnovato.com) strives to live by faith, be known by love and be a voice of hope in our community. My hope is your faith journey helps you achieve greater balance in life and *Success With People*.

Please note I alternate between using "he" and "she" to provide a reminder that both men and women can be effective managers.

Why You Should Read This Book

Did you start your business or are you a manager primarily because you wanted to manage people?

When I am speaking before a group and ask this question, most people laugh and shout, "No!" Yet managing people effectively is the only way to succeed long-term in business.

Success With People **is a system for hiring the right people and managing them to achieve their best.** Thousands of people have used aspects of this system to create millions of dollars in wealth. *You can too!*

My understanding is UCLA performed a study years ago and determined the average seminar attendee forgets 93 percent of what he learns within 72 hours. If this is the case, then information by itself does not make you a better manager. You need a flexible system for managing people effectively.

This book shares my unique winning system. Here are 10 reasons why you should read this book:

Reason #1: Leverage What Others Have Proven

Enclosed is a proven system for managing people based on three suites of *Desired Results*:

- ❑ Establish Your Foundation
- ❑ Balance Your Workload
- ❑ Manage Your Team's Performance

Success With People is referred to as a "proven system" because I have personally talked and/or worked with dozens of people who attribute their success managing others to systematically using these *Desired Results*.

Learn and use this system for success. This book is different because it proposes a foundational <u>system</u> of people management rather than just some <u>ideas</u>.

A 2005 Accenture ad states, *"There comes a time when execution is more important than theory."* This is a reminder why a <u>complete</u> system is so important.

Reason #2: Save Time

You can save at least 10 hours a year per employee you manage when you use this system rather than managing haphazardly.

Do the math. If the *Success With People* system saves you a fraction of that time, it is worth reading this book.

Reason #3: Increase Productivity

I recently consulted with a $50 million company. Based on the president's estimates, the company was losing $700,000 annually in lost employee productivity. How much is lost productivity costing you? *If you are curious, email me. I have a spreadsheet that can calculate it for you.*

Often lost productivity costs your company half or more of your net profits. <u>It is the annual cost of doing nothing.</u> Read this book and then use my system. There are human resources professionals with decades of experience telling me this system is right on target and it is even giving them new ideas.

Reason #4: Avoid Litigation

The average cost to settle an employee lawsuit today is $300,000-$500,000.[2] The Society of Human Resource Management is the largest association of HR professionals with over 160,000 members (www.SHRM.org). Recently <u>57% of survey respondents said an employee had sued them during the prior year</u>.[3]

Nothing eliminates all possible liabilities, but this system helps you manage more effectively plus document employee behavior quickly and easily so lawsuits can be avoided.

The government collects hundreds of millions in fines from businesses just like yours every year. The Wage and Hour Division of the U.S. Department of Labor collected $212,537,554 in 2003 for unpaid overtime. Total employee discrimination claims added another $300,000,000 more in fines.

The most recent figure I can find is there are 18 MILLION LAWSUITS (civil, not criminal) pending in the courts today.[4] I believe thousands of companies find themselves out of business each year due to an employee lawsuit. Avoid being one of them in part by protecting your company with a proven system for managing employees.

Reason #5: Improve Effectiveness

The *Success With People* system improves your own effectiveness with the managers reporting to you, assuming you teach them this proven systematic approach to managing people.

Executives regularly tell me that since they started using my system, their employees are thanking them for their performance reviews. This success results from writing more informative reviews (in less time) and making the review part of a year-round management system (*Halftime Reviews – Desired Result #11*).

How much additional profit would you be enjoying if your people were more effectively managed?

Reason #6: Hire The Right People

Hiring people is costly and takes a lot of time. In *Right Person – Right Job* (*Desired Result #7*), you learn how to hire the best and avoid the rest.

I teach you a 10 step system to define your openings, promote them, qualify the candidate and bring them onboard in a manner that increases your retention rates. The impact on profits is huge.

Reason #7: Retain Your Best People

According to Dr. Pierre Mornell, as quoted in Nations Business, *"When an employee leaves you... you're going to lose 2 1/2 times the person's annual salary, whether they're entry-level or senior management."*[5]

According to Cornell University the total cost of losing a single hourly employee is 30 percent of their annual salary. According to the Saratoga Institute, and independently verified by Hewitt Associates, the cost for salaried employees can be 150 percent of their annual salary.[6] Other estimates are as high as $1 million to replace an employee whose total compensation is only $75,000 – and that estimate is from the company itself, not a researcher.[7]

Employee turnover is expensive any way you calculate the cost, yet *Success With People* helps you retain your best people.

Reason #8: Balance Personal / Professional Life

One of my goals is to help you enjoy a more balanced life. I have over 30 years business experience and have talked with hundreds of experts to learn their secrets to success. I have read hundreds of books and articles on how to manage people and priorities. I have tested dozens of methods to identify what works best.

Life is too short to spend your time all on business activities. My mission is to *help you succeed by managing people and priorities more effectively* so you have more time for your personal pursuits.

Reason #9: Motivate Your Team

The Gallup Organization reports only 25% of employees are engaged at work,[8] estimating disengaged workers cost American business $292 to $355 billion a year.

Increase the motivation of your employees by using this system to get them more engaged in your business.

How much more revenue will your team generate if your employees are just 10 percent more motivated? *The amount will be substantially more than the cost of this book!*

Reason #10: Improve Your Business

This system works for all types and sizes of businesses wherever your company is located.

Is it more important to be an effective leader or manager? <u>Leaders set direction whereas managers deliver results</u>. Both are important, but develop people management skills if you have to choose between the two.   As you improve results as a manager, you simultaneously demonstrate leadership skills and abilities.

Many leaders at companies worldwide are laying-off workers and exporting jobs to foreign countries. Many top executives believe they do not have to manage people better. They can ship the work overseas and often make a higher bonus as a result.

Shipping too many jobs overseas has big risks. Here are 3 of them:

- ❑ The actual savings are about 20 percent – *and often <u>you can save that by managing people more effectively</u>.*

- ❑ Your overseas "partner" <u>often becomes your competitor</u>.

- ❑ If you ship jobs overseas, <u>who is left to buy your products</u> in America?

Responsible companies are balancing hiring internationally with developing their American workers to remain competitive. For instance Honda, a Japanese company, is exporting some jobs from Japan to Marysville, Ohio. USA Today reports the 16,000 Honda jobs in Ohio have <u>created a total of 128,000 jobs</u> in the area as Honda worker paychecks get spread around the local economy.[9]

Think how many more people would have a job in America if senior executives, shareholders and elected government officials were fully committed to developing and managing American citizens into becoming the world's most effective workforce.

"If we want jobs in our country, we need to manage people better," according to Jim Finkelstein of FutureSense. America must correct its inefficiencies, not just ship them overseas.

Lead by Serving

High performing managers and employees ultimately determine the long-term success of any organization. The leader who has an attitude of serving her customers, employees and shareholders is the most effective executive long-term.

Part of the foundation of people management was established for America in its political structure. If you want to be reminded of two great servant politicians, then read *Theodore Rex,*[10]about Teddy Roosevelt by Edmund Morris, and *John Adams*, by David McCullough.[11]

If you want *Success With People* then serve your employees, customers and shareholders first before yourself. Jim Collins' study that became the best-selling book, *Good to Great,* also confirmed this enduring truth. Success comes through serving.

Serving others includes humbly helping your people achieve objectives on their own rather than doing the work yourself. This involves a disciplined, systematic approach to train, coach and motivate your team for success. Your activities demonstrate the core values of your business[12] and then your people extend those values to your customers.

True knowledge *is understanding the processes that deliver success, and then demonstrating that knowledge through your actions.* This book explains the proven *Success With People* system, but to have a positive impact on your company you must use the system and teach it to others.

If you need help or want to learn more, visit our web site at www.SuccessWithPeople.com. It contains valuable (free and subscription) content, information on our executive coaching programs and other tools to assist you in your quest for success.

I recommend you grab a highlighter pen to identify the parts of *Success With People* that are most meaningful to you. Then reviewing your favorite sections in the future is much easier.

Executive Summary

Here is a quick overview of the *Success With People* system.

<u>Establish Your Foundation</u>

1. *Systematic Power* is a commitment to hire, manage, develop and retain talent systematically.

2. *Understand How You Make a Difference* makes working for your company a meaningful experience and fuels employee passion to achieve.

3. *LOI: Live It - Observe It - Improve It* involves your employees with your products to increase their passion for your company and ability to serve clients better.

4. *Sanctuary* combines *Rest, Reflect,* and *Risk* to give you a clearer perspective, renewed energy and inspirational creativity to achieve your best.

<u>Balance Your Workload</u>

5. *Success Plans* help you achieve key goals by balancing personal and professional objectives more effectively.

6. *Pass The Baton on Job Responsibilities* efficiently delegates work to your employees.

7. *Right Person – Right Job* is a complete, proven hiring system to hire the best and avoid the rest.

8. *Compensation That Pays* motivates your people by paying them as co-owners while demonstrating company values through your actions.

9. *Listen More* involves regular interaction with employees to learn from them, show appreciation and document behavior to support promotions or dismissals.

10. *Goals That Work* is a proven method for setting clear goals and following-up consistently to achieve maximum success.

11. *Halftime Reviews* transform performance reviews from a once-a-year agony to a motivational meeting that confirms employee past performance and their next bold moves.

12. *Coach – Do Not Play* is teaching your people to think on their own so they become better at their work than you.

Establish Your Foundation

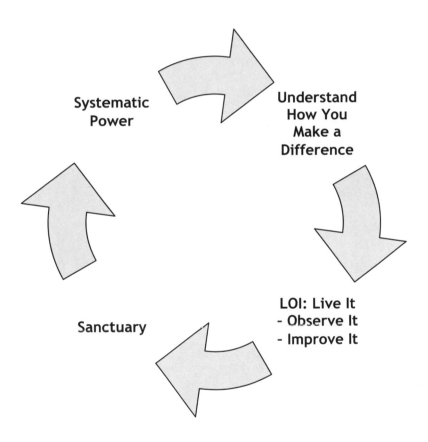

Systematic Power

Understand How You Make a Difference

LOI: Live It
- Observe It
- Improve It

Sanctuary

Systematic Power

You can become a master of managing people. Masters still make mistakes, but *masters accept that achievement is a disciplined effort, an ongoing process, and a lifelong journey of learning.*

It is easy to become a master of your success with others if you follow an effective system of managing people and continue your learning process to further exploit the power of the proven system.

The first *Desired Result* of *Success With People* is *Systematic Power* because a successful business is managed around systems proven to be efficient, effective, and profitable. One of the most important systems is how you manage people.

Managing others more effectively increases your company profits, creates new career opportunities for you, and positively impacts people who rely on you for leadership.

The starting point for your business systems must be how you select, train, and manage your people because everything else you attempt to accomplish is affected by these decisions.

Help your people understand the importance of leveraging systems to build greater efficiency and effectiveness into all their activities. Just as a vegetable garden is regular work and rewards (sowing and reaping), continuously develop the capabilities of your people and systems to achieve your objectives.

One added benefit of this system of managing talent provides new knowledge that enables your company to compete more effectively by improving your development, sales and support efforts.

The benefits of the *Success With People* system go beyond helping you increase your income and enabling your company to achieve higher profits. As a member of a global economy, **you are fighting for your way of life.**

A nation's competitive edge is based on its ingenuity and productivity. For hundreds of thousands of Americans this means you must improve your productivity by managing people and resources more effectively or your job is headed to a competitor or overseas.

Why does *Success With People* emphasize a system rather than just giving you 1001 ideas to manage people better?

Management tips are for people seeking an answer to a specific employee management problem. For instance, you may have a worker who is tardy often and you want to know how to motivate him to show up to work on time. Or two workers are not getting along and you need tips on how to mediate the situation. For situations like these you need tips, ideas, and information that you can implement within a system.

In contrast, a system is a series of actions proven to be effective at achieving a task such as managing people. A system involves tools, knowledge, software, equipment, and/or step-by-step procedures. The key qualification of the system is it has demonstrated itself to be successful. *A proven system enables you to achieve the maximum possible gain.*

For example, have you ever considered the systems continuously developed to maximize the profits of a quick serve restaurant, such as a McDonalds or Taco Bell?

Some quick serve restaurant chains are experts at training their franchisees on business systems to maximize employee performance, effectiveness, and profits. Recently I ran across a businessman who used to work for a very well respected company with about 3,000 employees. I asked him what he was doing now.

He explained he was working for another company, but part-time he and his wife had purchased 9 Taco Bell franchise stores. He went on to say prior to purchasing his first Taco Bell franchise, he expected to bring a lot of business expertise to the organization. He was surprised after they purchased the stores to discover none of his knowledge was needed. Taco Bell does such a great job of establishing proven systems to operate their stores there was nothing upon which he could improve.

Furthermore, the systems established by quick serve restaurants are always being reviewed, improved upon, and trained to the next generation of managers. I remember being in a McDonalds restaurant years ago and hearing the manager talking with a management trainee. He was saying the labor cost of the store the prior month was a certain percentage, and it should be 2 percent less. He then explained to the trainee the steps they would take to bring that cost down so they were maximizing profits.

Sustained success is never simple. You have to work hard, but more importantly work smart. The people who make the most money long-term are typically disciplined people who wisely defined their system of success and work that system day after day. They may not have invented the system for success, but they apply it to their business, refine it, and continue to work and improve the system.

In the book, *Good to Great,*[13] Jim Collins identifies several companies that grew substantially after years of very little growth. One of the key reasons this happened was each company identified how they made money most effectively and then worked the system.

It is important to recognize you have to use the entire system for maximum effectiveness. You cannot pull off one piece and expect great results. A true system *is a chain of cascading events where one feeds off the next.*

WARNING: Do not allow yourself to be distracted into old ineffective habits or back into the daily grind of work you do today. If this is a concern, get a coach. A coach is a low cost method of accelerating your progress towards success. To learn about our executive coaching or low-cost *Success With People Club*, visit our web site.

The *Success With People* system requires a reasonable amount of discipline to succeed just as dieting, exercising, saving for retirement, and other significant goals. People accomplish key objectives every day. You can too.

Before we go further, please recognize you need basic work rules in place for your people to make the most of your systems – and for your company to be compliant with federal and state laws.

You need a policy manual to define the rules under which your employees work. Most companies have an incomplete, out-of-date policy manual, or one so thick employees do not bother to read it.

If you get into an employee dispute and the employee sues your company, the first thing the courts often ask for is a copy of the company *policy manual* to determine if the employee actually has a valid claim. In the absence of clear written policies, the company is often found to be at fault because you cannot demonstrate the claim is without cause.

For instance, an employee could threaten to sue your company because of a dispute with his manager regarding working overtime. If you have a clear policy mandating both the manager and employee must sign-off on the timecard for overtime, the employee has a much more challenging task to prove his case.

Unfortunately an employee can sue you even if you have good policies in place. The difference is good written policies limit your legal costs, time spent on defending against the litigation and the harm to your business.

Policies are important to your productivity. Gossip and distraction generated from someone violating a company policy, such as sexual harassment, can cause a temporary 20 percent dip in productivity or as much as a 30 percent drop if the case makes the local papers or television news. [14]

Hiring an attorney to write your policy manual is an expensive but thorough option. I know an HR consultant who was paid $30,000 to write a policy manual for a client. Each policy manual can be different based on your business and the state your business operates.

Policies Now software enables you to follow a simple question and answer process to write a custom policy manual for your firm. One person claimed it saved him 40 hours of work. It costs less than $200 and meets the needs of most companies.

We used the software to write an entire policy manual unique to our company in less than 2 hours. It has over 90 policies. We just selected the policies we wanted, answered the questions, and it wrote the policies for us.

Here are some thoughts as to why a policy manual is important:

- ❑ It is critical to understand the difference between policies and procedures. Policies involve compliance with Federal and State employment laws. A policy may involve a procedure, such as how to apply for maternity leave, but its focus is to explain an aspect of employment. In contrast processes or procedures are written to explain how to accomplish tasks according to your standards.

- ❑ Just having a policy manual does not enable you to avoid or win all employee lawsuits. The government expects a company to build a culture that encourages commitment to the law. You have to actively prevent violations. When a violation occurs, your company must demonstrate action and document the situation.

- ❑ Policy manuals typically set the rules of employment so your people understand your dress code, vacation days, holidays, benefits, smoking rules, and other guidelines you have set forth for your work environment. A well-written policy manual helps you hold people accountable to these rules in a consistent manner.

- ❑ If you are writing your first policy manual, share a draft at a company meeting or via email prior to producing the final version. This provides employees an opportunity to comment on it, which communicates you want them involved and accountable.

- ❑ If your company has a huge policy manual already, then review the key policies with your team. Encourage them to read the rest on their own – particularly since they all should have signed a document confirming they had read and agreed to your policies.

❑ Review your policy manual with employees annually to discuss any changes and the key sections. It does not take a lot of time, but does reinforce the fact there are certain rules your company has established for the benefit of employees. You can make it a fun question and answer game complete with inexpensive prizes. Have your employees sign a document they have reviewed the policy manual including any changes. Keep this signed document in their employment file.

❑ Keep your employee file drawer locked. Your company may be like a family today, but all it takes is one unhappy employee to steal their documentation when no one is around to cause a major problem.

Systematic Power is not about policies, but policies provide a support structure for your systems. *Systematic Power* is about how to run your business and manage people effectively.

Cisco CEO, John Chambers, is urging his solution providers to become experts on business processes. IBM CEO, Sam Palmisano, is promoting business process as a critical driver for the future.[15] To compete in today's economy you have to constantly improve your systems to create greater efficiency and effectiveness.

Systematic Power is not a fad. It is a survival and wealth generating business essential.

Here are three quick benefits of using systems:

1. Systems are proven to maximize efficiencies within a business when they are constantly evolving;

2. Systems transfer knowledge and skill through a series of actions proven to achieve results;

3. Proven, evolving systems are effective. *Efficiency is about getting results in less time. Effectiveness means the system delivers the best results* in the least amount of time to meet customer needs.

16

You use systems or processes in many areas of your company. **Why not with people?**

Consider Nike's story as told in the Harvard Business Review.[16] Studying their history explains how Nike has leveraged systems to expand into new markets.

Years ago Nike's entry into the golf market appeared to be impossible. They had no products for the golf market at all. But those who had followed the company closely over the previous decade were not surprised. They recognized the system Nike had applied and adapted successfully in a series of entries into sports markets – from jogging to volleyball to tennis to basketball to soccer.

Nike begins by establishing a leading position in athletic shoes in the target market. Next, Nike launches a clothing line endorsed by the sport's top athletes – like Tiger Woods, whose $100 million deal in 1996 gave Nike the visibility it needed to get traction in golf apparel and accessories. Expanding into new categories allows the company to forge new distribution channels and lock in suppliers. Then it starts to feed higher-margin equipment into the market – irons first, in the case of golf clubs, and subsequently drivers. In the final step, Nike moves beyond the U.S. market to global distribution.

Systems work for companies of all sizes and are critical for you to sustain success as soon as you get beyond 3-5 employees. The *Success With People* system is a proven process for managing employees and balancing your workload.

More than hard work the *Success With People* system takes discipline. It can be mentally or emotionally challenging, but only because of distractions we allow into our workday and bad habits we have developed. Avoid shortcuts. The rewards are worth it.

As the old saying goes, *"If you can't measure it, you can't manage it."* One final benefit of *Systematic Power* is your systems provide reporting on how your people are performing so managers make better decisions.

For instance, imagine your company is trying to improve customer service. The *Success With People* system enables managers to measure the ability of employees to deliver excellent customer service. You can then increase employee training and/or revise policies or procedures based on the statistical, documented performance of your customer service team.

The next *Desired Result, Understand How You Make a Difference*, moves *Systematic Power* into overdrive by developing passion in your employees.

Conclusion

Historically the starting point to construct a building was to establish cornerstones at the four corners of the foundation to provide strength to the structure. The foundation was not strong enough to withstand the weather without the cornerstones.

The *Success With People* system starts with the four *Desired Results* of the *Establish Your Foundation* suite, which are comparable to the cornerstones of a building's foundation.

The entire *Success With People* system can be viewed as a 12-step program to manage others effectively. I refer to each step as a *Desired Result*. Some of the *Desired Results* are used only occasionally, so *do not be overwhelmed.* You are in control of how to implement the system.

The first *Desired Result* cornerstone of the *Establish Your Foundation* suite is:

1. *Systematic Power* is a commitment to hire, manage, develop and retain talent systematically.

Each of these *Desired Results* work together daily. The level of your commitment to a system for managing people effectively affects everything you do at work.

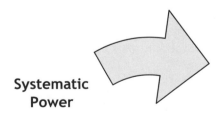

Systematic Power

Systematic Power is a commitment to hire, manage, develop and retain talent systematically. Here is a quick summary.

✓ Commit yourself to establish systems for accomplishing key tasks in your company, especially a system for managing people.

✓ Communicate the power of systems to your people. Often.

✓ Be disciplined. Live by _Systematic Power_ more than talk about it. Evaluate your actions weekly during _Sanctuary_ (_Desired Result #4_) to confirm you are working the system.

✓ Document key processes; train your people on them; improve the processes; repeat this process.

✓ Write, maintain, and communicate your company policies. If you do not have a policy manual or need to update one, save time by using software for writing a policy manual in less than 2 hours if needed.

Understand How You Make a Difference

How much do you love your work? If you do not love your work, why are you doing it? To know success in life means to spend your life doing something that is meaningful to you and makes you come alive.

This is also the key to fully engaging your employees - a large part of loving your work is feeling there is meaning in what you do and that your work has a positive impact on each one of your customers and/or your community.

A crucial component of effective employee management is to *Understand How You Make a Difference*. This is the second *Desired Result* cornerstone of the *Establish Your Foundation* suite you are building. Your employees love their work when they understand why your company's products and/or services improve the lives of your customers. Success is about significance more than money.

Part of helping your people *Understand How You Make a Difference* is clearly communicating your business strategy and involving them in decisions. This gives them ownership and provides additional insight into the best possible solutions.

When your employees understand your business strategy and the positive impact it has on your customers, they identify areas where they can contribute that are outside of their traditional job responsibilities. Your company, customers and employees all benefit from this extra effort.

Communicate regularly how your company is positively impacting the lives of others and listen to employee responses. *Do not just go through the motions.* <u>Really consider the responses</u>. *Listen More* sincerely to set an example for employees and encourage them to listen to ideas from customers and fellow team members.

In the end, <u>the only opinion that matters is the customer's.</u> Understanding this and creating the best products to meet customer needs makes work exciting.

Ask questions <u>before</u> you make decisions

Involve your employees in key decisions when those decisions impact their responsibilities and/or lives. This helps validate their contribution to the company and enables you to make the best choices. Select the right time to bring an employee into a conversation because it often varies with the person.

Business Week reported on a poll by the AFL-CIO Professional Employee Department of 1,200 non-union nurses, tech workers, and university faculty. These people wanted a collective voice in their workplace <u>more than better salaries and benefits</u>.[17]

Make certain you listen to employee comments, then either adopt their suggestion or explain your reasoning not to use the idea. You still make the decision, but sincerely considering the opinions of your team and explaining your conclusion is important.

Do you think this sounds like too much work? Is life just too busy? Then consider this: Have decisions ever been made at your company where you felt the solution would have been better if someone had seriously considered your opinion?

When your company makes a decision without consulting you and the decision is not the best, part of your love for your work is lost. Do you understand why?

When you know your products or services are not as good as they can be your work becomes less meaningful.

Do you feel the power in these words? Effective managers make certain their people are actively involved in doing meaningful work. It is a critical way for you to serve your employees, company, and ultimately your customers.

Think about it: If you worked for Mother Teresa, <u>you would know</u> your efforts helped save human lives. *In contrast, the value a company delivers to customers is not so easily understood in many jobs.* You have to help your people understand and then reinforce it regularly.

For instance, what is so great about working at your local convenience store? The typical employee turnover rate in this business exceeds 100 percent annually, but who said you have to be "typical?"

Recently the Harvard Business Review[18] reported on QuickTrip and Wawa, two privately-held companies that each operates over 400 convenience stores. The employee turnover rate at typical convenience stores easily exceeds 100 percent, yet the rates at these firms are 14 and 22 percent respectively. How do they do it?

Here is my perspective on some of the key areas they do well.

- ❑ *Understand How You Make a Difference*: They live their values, including not selling lottery tickets (Wawa) and being a leader in removing porn magazines (QT).

- ❑ *LOI: Live It - Observe It - Improve It*: Their entire organizations are dedicated to be the best and that commitment drives the passion of their employees.

- ❑ *Right Person – Right Job*: They hire in a manner that is consistent with the *Success With People* system.

- ❑ *Compensation That Pays*: They share financial information with employees to help them make better decisions and pay people based on performance.

- ❑ *Listen More*: They work hard to learn from customers and share ideas on how to improve their brand. It is a community effort.

- ❑ *Coach – Do Not Play*: They view their employees as an important asset to be retained and developed.

I believe their core strengths are the way they live their values and develop community among both employees and customers.

These two companies communicate their values by their actions with employees and customers. The results are the highest profits in the industry.

PLEASE UNDERSTAND this does not mean these companies are full of like-minded people. The people manning the stores, those in the warehouse, and others in the corporate office are all different. Their work environment or culture varies also. <u>The difference is everyone is emotionally engaged in the mission and values of the company</u>.

When I meet people in a non-business setting so often they dismiss their ability to manage people better because their particular business is construction, painting, accounting, or something else that is not a current fad or high-tech.

QT and Wawa prove you do not have to be in a glamorous business to succeed. It is not complicated. It just means you have to develop a systematic approach to your business that demonstrates your values through your actions – *and then do it!*

Walk, do not talk your mission

Does your company have a mission statement? Can you say it from memory? (Most people cannot.)

<u>Your mission statement defines the value your company delivers to your customers</u>. It should state this succinctly. It not only communicates value to your customers, but also provides a simple benchmark against which your employees may consider their daily decisions. It helps reinforce why their work has meaning each day. Some companies have ineffective long mission statements. It is more powerful to have a brief mission statement every employee can state from memory because knowing it better enables them to live it each day.

If your large corporation has a long mission statement, one option is to craft a shorter version for your team. It should be consistent with your overall organizational mission statement. Perhaps you can take one word from each sentence of your company's mission statement and make those words the mission statement for your team.

Here are some sample mission statements.

Sample Mission Statements

To provide the most useful and ethical financial services in the world.

The Charles Schwab Company[19]

To be the global energy company most admired for its people, partnership and performance.

Chevron[20]

The mission of the Boy Scouts of America is to prepare young people to make ethical and moral choices over their lifetimes by instilling in them the values of the Scout Oath and Law.

Boy Scouts of America[21]

To enable people and businesses throughout the world to realize their full potential.

Microsoft[22]

To unleash the potential and power of people and organizations for the common good.

The Ken Blanchard Companies[23]

Some managers also encourage employees to write individual, personal mission statements for their company role. These can be very empowering if people are encouraged to live them each day.

There are many ways to create your mission statement. Franklin Covey has a free mission statement writer on their web site. Here are two simple examples from *The Dream Giver Coach Network (www.thedreamgivercoachnetwork.com)*.[24]

I   support   _____   in   their   desire   to
_____ by means of _____.

Example: I support <u>mothers</u> in their desire to <u>find</u>
<u>their dream</u> by means of <u>asking clarifying</u>
<u>questions</u>.

I   _____   with   _____   who
_____ because _____.

Example: I <u>strategize</u> with <u>women</u> who <u>want a more</u>
<u>organized and balanced life</u> because <u>it is</u>
<u>easier to achieve your goals with a</u>
<u>partner</u>.

Why not take a moment right now to write your own **personal mission** statement? Come up with something that works for you. Please limit the length of your statement. It can be as short as one word, such as: Love.

Next write your own **personal values** statement. This might be called, *My Governing Values*, because the objective is to describe behaviors that communicate your personal beliefs. Keep it in a place where you can see it often. When you review it, try to slow down and *Reflect* on each item.

On the next page is a sample of my governing values. *This sample is available free on our web site.* Yes, it does mention my faith. If you have spiritual beliefs, they should be an important component of your personal values. If you do not believe in God, then obviously having a value pertaining to faith would be a lie. These values are important to me. Yours will be different.

My Governing Values

Faith
I am unwavering in my belief in Jesus Christ. He has proven Himself to me. I pray daily. I pause and take time to consider "what would Jesus do?" prior to making decisions. I memorize verses of Scripture to help me to interact with others as Jesus did *- in love, with patience, and respect.*

Integrity

I do not exaggerate. I do not make business decisions that put the capital of others at unnecessary risk. I do what I say I will do. I am honest in my communication and actions.

Gratitude

I am thankful for all things occurring in my life including the challenges, unmet expectations, daily blessings, family members, and others who encourage me. I pause daily to reflect on my blessings and say thanks to God.

Fun

I have fun and laugh every day. I organize, help organize and support events that give opportunities for others to have fun.

Work Smart

I work smart and hard in everything I do. I invest an adequate amount of time prior to a project to plan it thoroughly, and then implement the plan.

Loving

I demonstrate love every day to others. I love my wife by helping at home, hugs, and complimenting her. I love our children by giving them my time, attention, encouragement, phone calls when away, and time together. I love Mom by regularly contacting her and being with her. I love others by identifying and reinforcing something positive I see in them.

Personal Growth

I live each day as a learning experience recognizing the fact I have much to learn. I exercise at least 3 times a week. I read.
I work on growing as a couple.

Listening

I am a patient, caring, attentive listener, growing in my ability to more carefully consider and evaluate what others have to say.

Encouragement

I am a positive encourager to all people at all times, including during times of correction, training, discipline, and disrespect towards me. I never lose hope. Jesus always comes through.

Family

I love my family. I devote time to my family instead of other activities. I do my best to protect, train, and serve each family member.

Success

I only invest my time in activities that are meaningful beyond any cash compensation.

Financial Freedom

I am committed to be debt free.

A few thoughts on Your Governing Values

1. Write them as though you are doing them. This trains your mind and conscience. You will not be perfect and live every aspect of your life according to your values, but if you word them that "I try" to do this or "I strive" to do that, you mentally encourage yourself to fail. Please consider structuring your *Governing Values* as absolutes for your life rather than weak suggestions.

    For instance, do you strive to be honest or are you honest? Do you try to exercise 3 times a week, or are you doing it? Make the commitment or do not include the behavior as a *Governing Values* statement. Without the commitment this is a waste of time.

    PLEASE NOTE: No human lives their values 100% of the time. *It is impossible for an imperfect being to behave perfectly all the time.* Yet my experience has been that my life is more fulfilling and loving to others when I try my best to live by my values.

2. Make your values personal. (Individual family member names are removed from my example.) Please consider including specific family names in yours. At the end of the day, at the end of your life, the question of whether you lived your life in a meaningful way is determined by your actions and your relationship with other people.

Many people have said one way they determine if a potential new employee is a good hire is how that person treats others below them on the economic ladder. For instance, how do they interact with a waitress, receptionist, or doorman? In a similar way, how you treat your family and friends speaks loudly to what your personal values truly are.

3. Review and *Reflect* on them weekly or even daily if you prefer. Remind yourself of how you want to live your life and then it is easier to make decisions according to your values more consistently.

4. Hold yourself accountable to them. If you are really sincere about it, have someone else hold you accountable. (Ideally you can hold them accountable too.) Just be encouraging and respectful, yet firm.

Actions demonstrate values, not words

Does your company have a values statement? A values statement defines how a company operates.

Too often values statements are written to impress people rather than establish standards of behavior. Consider the questionable behavior by Ken Lay of Enron, Richard Grasso of the New York Stock Exchange, and Dennis Kozlowski of Tyco. Each of these organizations have great company values statements. Nevertheless the primary focus of these leaders was their own personal profit and their board of directors did not do their job. *There are thousands of disillusioned workers because leaders boast values but their actions violate the values they preach.*

For instance, a consultant was working with an East Coast company on how values impact their workforce and customers. In one of his training programs with executives, a participant described how his employees demonstrate the value of commitment.

With great satisfaction one executive told a story of how the company was recently overflowing with orders during the Christmas season. This executive proudly explained how all his supervisors agreed to work through the Christmas holidays and give up vacations because they were so committed. This was his interpretation of the events and definition of committed employees.

Later my friend interviewed the supervisors who work for this executive. One supervisor, when asked to describe the value of commitment used the same example, but with a radically different interpretation and outcome of events.

This woman gave up her holiday even though she and her husband had planned for months to take a 2-week vacation to visit their daughter and new grandchild in California. She was really looking forward to this vacation, but did not feel she had the option to refuse to work over the holiday unless she was willing to lose her job.

Her husband went on the vacation alone. One day after returning from California, he dropped dead of a heart attack. This woman will never forgive the company for what she feels was a corporate expectation that forced her to work. The company states it values employees, but it accidentally communicated to this employee that the company primarily cares about making money.

The point: It is very important to translate organizational values through your actions. Here is one way to look at it:

$$\frac{\textbf{Mission + Values}}{\textbf{Actions}} = \textbf{Results}$$

How you live your values (or not) affects the way your employees work. If your top executives are not living your company values through their actions, then management makes decisions without talking to customers or staff. Product development determines product features without talking with customer service, sales or customers. Worst of all, top management may earn big bonuses while other employees struggle to pay their bills.

What happens next is employees start stealing from your company. Not visibly taking things, but becoming so frustrated that some take the system for all they can. People take long breaks, surf the web for fun, make personal phone calls during work hours, and wander from cubicle to cubicle chatting about personal interests.

In a typical business today 25 percent of the employees do not enjoy their work, 50 percent do just enough to get by, and the remaining 25 percent carry the enthusiasm, and often the results, for the entire company.

Worse than that, 25 percent of workers *are just showing up to collect a paycheck"* and *"only 14% say they are very satisfied with their job,"* according to a Conference Board study.[25]

Part of this problem is because too many employees do not understand the value their company brings to their community, do not feel appreciated, and/or do not get along with their manager. The sad part is most of these people prefer to be really engaged and effective at work.

Recently James Clifton, CEO of Gallup, Inc. said, *"One of the things you notice in Gallup research is that* **only one in four workers in the U.S. are engaged in the workplace.** *It is just unbelievable to me the potential that exists for companies.*

"Imagine if they could even get half the employees engaged. I think a movement here could be a lot bigger than lean management, six sigma or even TQM."[26]

My experience and research indicates this "movement" starts with a system for managing people more effectively – the *Success With People* system.

After *Systematic Power*, the first step to realizing the potential of your employees is to make certain they *Understand How You Make a Difference.* This means your employees need to clearly understand how their actions and your solutions help your customers live better lives.

For instance, imagine the impact on your profits if you could move your people from 25 percent engagement, as James Clifton of Gallup states on the previous page, to 50 percent of your employees being actively engaged at work.

Your company is then operating at only 50 percent efficiency, yet you have <u>doubled productivity</u>!

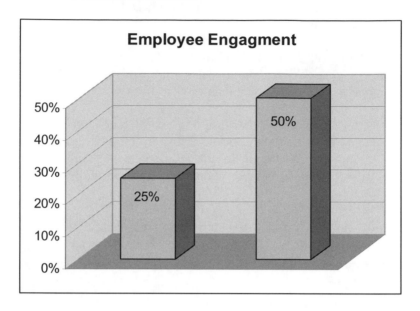

Sustained productivity gains all start with engaging your people by helping them *Understand How You Make a Difference.*

The following pages contain some examples of values statements.

Sample Values Statements

Starbucks[27]

Starbucks Mission Statement and Guiding Principles
To establish Starbucks as the premier purveyor of the finest coffee in the world while maintaining our uncompromising principles as we grow.

The following six Guiding Principles will help us measure the appropriateness of our decisions:

- Provide a great work environment and treat each other with respect and dignity.

- Embrace diversity as an essential component in the way we do business.

- Apply the highest standards of excellence to the purchasing, roasting and fresh delivery of our coffee.

- Develop enthusiastically satisfied customers all of the time.

- Contribute positively to our communities and our environment.

- Recognize that profitability is essential to our future success.

NOTE: It is interesting Starbucks goes beyond just writing their mission and values. They structure processes to hold themselves accountable, such as encouraging feedback from all employees ("partners"). *"One such option is Mission Review, which partners use to question whether or not Starbucks actions are consistent with our Mission Statement and Guiding Principles."*

Dell[28]

Many people are familiar with Dell's customer-focused direct business model, and the company's success in creating leading value for customers and investors. Less well known is the unique environment forged by Michael Dell and the people of Dell since the company's founding in 1984.

We characterize that environment in a statement of corporate philosophy called the "Soul of Dell." It defines the kind of company we are and aspire to become, serves as a guide for our actions around the world, and ultimately forms the basis of our "winning culture."

Below are the core elements of the Soul of Dell:

Customers: We believe in creating loyal customers by providing a superior experience at a great value. We are committed to direct relationships, providing the best products and services based on standards-based technology, and outperforming the competition with value and a superior customer experience.

The Dell Team: We believe our continued success lies in teamwork and the opportunity each team member has to learn, develop and grow. We are committed to being a meritocracy, and to developing, retaining and attracting the best people, reflective of our worldwide marketplace.

Direct Relationships: We believe in being direct in all we do. We are committed to behaving ethically; responding to customer needs in a timely and reasonable manner; fostering open communications and building effective relationships with customers, partners, suppliers and each other; and operating without inefficient hierarchy and bureaucracy.

Global Citizenship: We believe in participating responsibly in the global marketplace. We are committed to understanding and respecting the laws, values and cultures wherever we do business; profitably growing in all markets; promoting a healthy business climate globally; and contributing positively in every community we call home, both personally and organizationally.

Winning: We have a passion for winning in everything we do. We are committed to operational excellence, superior customer experience, leading in the global markets we serve, being known as a great company and great place to work, and providing superior shareholder value over time.

ServiceMaster[29]

Objectives   The ServiceMaster philosophy is expressed in four objectives.

To honor God in all we do
We believe that every person — regardless of personal beliefs or differences — has been created in the image and likeness of God. We seek to recognize the dignity, worth and potential of each individual and believe that everyone has intrinsic worth and value. This objective challenges us to have commitment to truth and to deliver what we promise. It provides the basis for

our belief in servant leadership. It is not an expression of a particular religious belief, or a basis for exclusion. Rather, it is a mandate for inclusion, and a constant reminder for us to do the right thing in the right way.

To help people develop
At ServiceMaster, work is about developing, contributing and feeling the accomplishment of a job well done. ServiceMaster believes in not only empowering people, but also enabling them to succeed. By giving people the tools and training to develop, we increase their productivity and earnings, and enhance the dignity, self-respect and worth of each individual.

To pursue excellence
We continually seek better methods of delivering service and believe that every time we touch a customer's life, we should provide added value for that customer. Pursuing excellence means that we must know our customers, understand their needs and expectations, regularly listen to them and adjust our processes and procedures to more effectively serve them.

To grow profitably
By achieving economic success, we will have the resources to positively affect the lives of our shareholders, customers and associates. Profitability is a way to test and challenge us. Profitability, productivity and quality reflect added value for our customers, a fair return for our shareholders, and improved opportunity for our people.

General Electric[30]

For more than 125 years, GE has been admired for its performance and imaginative spirit. The businesses that we invent and build fuel the global economy and improve people's lives.

Today, we are 11 technology, services and financial businesses with more than 300,000 employees in 160 countries around the world.

What unifies us? Our Actions and Values.

What we do and how we work is distinctly GE. It's a way of thinking and working that has grounded our performance for decades. It's a way of talking about our work and ourselves that takes the best from our past and expresses it in the spirit and language of GE today.

It's about who we are, what we believe, where we're headed, how we'll get there. It's how we imagine, solve, build and lead.

Imagine.

From the very beginnings of our company, when Thomas Edison was changing the world with the power of ideas, GE has always stood for one capability above all others - the ability to imagine.

Imagine is a sense of possibility that allows for a freedom beyond mere invention. Imagine dares to be something greater.

At GE, Imagine is an invitation to dream and do things that you didn't know you could do.

Because at GE the act of imagining is fused with empowerment - the confidence that what we imagine, we can make happen.

Solve.

Every business has to have a reason to exist - a reason that answers the fundamental question of "why are we here?"

For GE, the big question has a simple answer: We exist to solve problems - for our customers, our communities and societies, and for ourselves.

Build.

From 0 to 60 in six seconds? Try zero to $5 billion in five years.

It's not so much a vision for our future - where we're headed is in many ways a reflection of where we've already been. It's not a destination. It's a quest. A quest for growth. And when we look to the future, we know that for us, there's only one way to get there. Build.

Lead.

Imagine. Solve. Build. Each of these is merely a word without one vital element. Lead.

GE is already synonymous with leadership. But with this mantle comes responsibility. And it's not just a responsibility to maintain the status quo or manage what worked yesterday. It's the bigger responsibility to change.

Because change is the essence of what it means to lead. It's a call to action that engages our unceasing curiosity, our passion, and our drive to be first in everything that we do.

We Are a Company to Believe In.

Imagine.
Build.
Solve.
Lead.

In the end, our success is measured not only by our ability to think big, dazzling thoughts, but by our commitment to sweat the small stuff that brings ideas to life. It's a way - thinking and doing - that has been at the heart of GE for years.

The worth of this framework is how we translate it into our own personal work ethic and then extend it to our teams, businesses, cultures and different regions of the world. It's permission to cast aside any approach that seems dated - to imagine, solve, build and lead a better way of doing things.

Values

While GE has always performed with integrity and values, each business generation expresses those values according to the circumstances of the times. Now more than ever the expression and adherence to values is vital.

More than just a set of words, these values embody the spirit of GE at its best. They reflect the energy and spirit of a company that has the solid foundation to lead change as business evolves. And they articulate a code of behavior that guides us through that change with integrity.

The words reflected here represent a revitalization of our values. They are a call to action that asks every GE employee to recommit to a common set of beliefs about how we work in our world today. And while some of these words are new in their expression, they are based on a continuum of how GE has grown and performed through generations.

They are our words and our values... in our own voice.

Passionate
Curious
Resourceful
Accountable
Teamwork
Committed
Open
Energizing

Always With Unyielding Integrity

38

Notice the great the way GE adapted their values to a graphic that folded-in-half fits easily in your pocket? What a great reminder of how GE people make a difference in the lives of others! Notice also how GE stresses *"always with unyielding integrity"* and *"We are a company to believe in."*

Cisco employees have the words of the Cisco Culture on the backside of their ID badges. Gwendolyn Young of Saint Joseph Mercy Health hospital in Detroit, Michigan always keeps her company values printed on a small card in her pocket <u>as a reminder that her work has meaning</u>. *What would happen if your employees had that much healthy pride in your company?*

The Power of Shared Values

We live in a society where almost anything goes. <u>We have lost the discipline and benefits of living by a shared set of values</u>.

Do not underestimate the power of your actions setting an example that management and all employees share the same company values. Living your mission and values fuels employee passion for the positive difference your company makes in the lives of others. Employees who can rely on their company to live its values over short-term profits have more peace-of-mind, confidence, joy and passion to see their company succeed.

Every system ultimately succeeds or fails based on the passion of the people. We hear a lot about money to motivate behavior, but money is only a momentary motivator or confirmation of your values. Operating your organization under a set of <u>values shared by all employees</u> sustains you through the lean times and expands your opportunities more abundantly during the good times.

Do your people think they make the world a better place? This belief is incredibly motivating.

Consider how The Fruit Guys (<u>www.fruitguys.com</u>) think they are changing the world. They deliver fresh fruit to offices as an alternative to the sugary sodas and fatty snack food found in most vending machines.

Chris Mittelstadt, the founder, explains, *"We like to think of our fruit as the 'water cooler' of the 21st century. A box of fresh fruit is like a box of fresh flowers. We're changing the world in many ways, but in particular from a health benefit standpoint because we provide fresh fruit that makes people both physically and mentally healthier. I love what we do. This business gets me out of bed in the morning!"*

5 Actions you can take to change your world.

Action #1 is to *Understand How You Make a Difference* by first reflecting on why you love your work. If you do not love your work, you have 3 options:

a) Change your perspective by identifying attributes of your job that you enjoy and focus on them;

b) Look upon your work as a service to God or people, and love it for that reason; or

c) Discover your real passion (other work) and go do it. Too much time is spent at work not to enjoy it.

Action #2 is to understand how your products and services improve the lives of your customers and fellow employees.

Action #3 is to write a bold mission statement that briefly and succinctly summarizes how your company provides value to your customers. (Encourage people to write a personal mission statement too!)

Action #4 is to have a values statement describing the values under which your company operates.

Action #5 is to live your mission and values each day. *Do not expect perfection, yet strive for it.*

Senator John McCain recently chastised business people for their lack of courage. *"Corporate America has taken significant blows to its reputation, because too many executives don't have the courage to stand up for what they know is right."*[31]

I encourage you to be courageous. Demonstrate high ethics and morals in all you do. If it causes a setback, then rejoice in the opportunity to learn from the situation. The setback will be temporary. Your organization will become stronger and achieve more by remaining true to your values.

One approach to writing mission and values statements is to meet individually with each of your team members. Make it casual. Let them know you want to discuss 5 questions and expect totally candid answers. Assure them no one will be fired or promoted based on their responses. <u>You want the truth</u>.

Try these 5 questions (or come up with your own).

1. What are the mission and values of this Company? (Please respond only from memory.)

2. What do you love about your job or this Company?

3. Please be candid, what do you wish were different about your job or this Company?

4. What value does our products and services provide our customers and community?

5. Do you use the products we sell - why or why not?

Use this information to write or revise your mission and values statements, and then train your people how your company is delivering value to your clients. Communicate your mission statement and values by your actions, *and occasionally by words.* Hold your employees accountable to doing the same. Holding them accountable may cause some minor setbacks, but long-term it makes your company stronger.

One idea is to distribute copies of your mission and values statements printed on high quality paper. Ask each manager to discuss your mission statement and values with her team and get all team members to sign it. Hang the signed copy of your values in a classy picture frame prominently in their work area. Refer to it on a regular basis.

Review your mission statement and values weekly on your own and monthly/quarterly with your team. Discuss it as one of the first items on your meeting agenda to communicate its importance. Ask yourself and your team if everyone's actions are consistent with your mission and values. Your mission may have to be adapted in the future due to changing business conditions. Only write what you can deliver.

Your people need to see customers being truly served, feel their concerns are being heard, and experience their needs being met. Then their inner hopes and needs for meaning each day can be achieved. A friend of mine, Joe (www.QuestNovato.com), commented recently, *"Hope is the heartbeat of the apprentice."*

You want your employees to always have hope, because hope enables us to continue in the face of adversity. Every business has challenges and tough times. Hope is significant in its relationship to your company's pursuit of sustained success and retaining your best employees.

Martin Luther King Jr. once encouraged us, *"We must accept finite disappointment, but never lose infinite hope."* The Bible is based on a hope God rewards those who seek Him. Our nation is founded upon the hope that people working together for a common good are more prosperous and fulfilled than people living under a selfish monarchy or dictatorship. Hope for a reward or better life is an incredible motivator. As Dr. King said, you should accept and even expect disappointment, but never lose hope or stop working for a better world.

Conclusion

Research from New York University School of Continuing and Professional Studies indicates frustrated workers crave more responsibility and meaning from their jobs. Almost 2-to-1 said they are motivated by greater fulfillment at work rather than money.[32]

Living your mission and values creates passion in your people as they *Understand How You Make a Difference*. Marti, the wife of John Fischer, www.PurposeDrivenLife.com Daily Devotional columnist, observes, *"It's not the big things you say, it's the little things you do."*

You now have learned the first two cornerstones to *Establish Your Foundation* for *Success With People*.

Establish Your Foundation

1. *Systematic Power* is a commitment to hire, manage, develop and retain talent systematically.

2. *Understand How You Make a Difference* makes working for your company a meaningful experience and fuels employee passion to achieve.

Each of these *Desired Results* work together. You can see how a system for managing talent increases your consistency and better develops your working relationships. Then add in living your commitment for meaningful work and the result is your employees become much more passionate about the work they are doing.

We are now halfway through *Establishing Your Foundation* and already the impact of just these two *Desired Results* is very significant on your company.

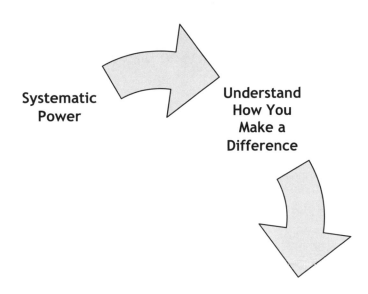

Systematic Power

Understand How You Make a Difference

Understand How You Make a Difference
makes working for your company a meaningful experience and fuels employee passion to achieve. Here is a quick summary.

- ✓ Write a simple mission statement with your people that everyone can rally around. Reinforce it. Live it. (See samples on page 25.)

- ✓ Write your values statement with your management team and try living it before announcing it. Then train your people how to live it and reinforce it. (See examples on page 32.)

- ✓ Choose to embrace your values over making excessive profits when that decision must be made.

- ✓ Avoid the temptation to act unethically that occurs in every business.

- ✓ Involve your people and customers in key decisions.

- ✓ Understand the value your company delivers to your community. Enhance and communicate this value regularly.

- ✓ Do the 5 Action Items starting on page 40.

- ✓ Remember:

$$\frac{\text{Mission} + \text{Values}}{\text{Actions}} = \text{Results}$$

LOI: Live It – Observe It – Improve It

Hope may be the heartbeat of the apprentice, but hope is also the lifeblood of any company. Your employees must have hope and faith their work is making a positive difference in the lives of other people for your organization to sustain success.

If your people do not *Understand How You Make a Difference*, then you probably have at least three problems:

❑ Your people are busy in their work just doing activities rather than achieving your key objectives.

❑ Some may be withholding a 100 percent effort because working at your company feels like a job with no future.

❑ Those people who *Understand How You Make a Difference* often assume everyone else shares their understanding. They just keep busy with their own responsibilities rather than communicate the good news about your solutions to others in the organization.

What is the answer? How do you get all your people to *Understand How You Make a Difference* and communicate it to everyone they meet?

The answer is your people must use your products so they intimately understand the quality and value your company delivers. They need the next cornerstone of the *Establish Your Foundation* suite - *LOI*, which is to *Live It* (use your solutions) – *Observe it* (observe others using your solutions and competitive products) – *Improve It* (improve your solutions constantly).

45

It is hypocritical to sell something as a good value when the product is not good enough for your own people to buy it and use it. Do you use your own products? To effectively sell something, you have to live with it yourself.

One part of helping your employees understand the value of your solutions is to create a table of features and benefits your solutions deliver. List the product at the top. Features are in the left column. The next columns list data on your solutions and those of your competitors. If your competitors have features or benefits not found in your products, list them but in your column explain how you plan to compensate for these missing features.

Have your team do the research. Assign people to fill in the blanks on each competitor, report the results to one person who organizes the data, and then discuss the information as a group.

Be careful not to get carried away watching the competition. Like a jockey riding in a horse race, your primary focus must always be on the finish line rather than the other riders. Create and manage your research on a regular basis as a detailed outline rather than a long, boring narrative. Update your competitive analysis every 3-6 months.

Talk to your customers as part of this process. Surveying the people who actually use your products daily is significantly more important than hearing the opinions from the senior executives of your client companies. Decision maker opinions deserve your respect, but *the actual users of your products provide the insights you need to compete.*

Seeing how your products are improving business processes and people's lives in real-life conditions is an excellent way for your employees to develop a passion for your products.

On the next page is one example of how to create these tables (this sample Microsoft Word document is available free on our web site):

WIDGET – COMPETITIVE ANALYSIS				Month/Year
Features and Functions	**Our Widget**	**Competitor #1**	**Competitor #2**	**Competitor #3**
Feature/Function	Description	Description	Description	Description
Feature/Function	Description	Description	Description	Description
Feature/Function	Description	Description	Description	Description
Area of Functionality				
Feature/Function	Yes	No	Yes	Yes
Feature/Function	Yes	No	Yes	Yes
Feature/Function	Yes	No	Yes	Yes
Feature/Function	Yes	No	Yes	Yes
Feature/Function	Yes	No	Yes	Yes
Feature/Function	Yes	No	Yes	Yes
Feature/Function	Yes	No	Yes	Yes
Area of Functionality				
Feature/Function	Yes	No	No	No
Feature/Function	No - due 2011	Yes	Yes	Yes
Feature/Function	Yes	No	No	No
Feature/Function	No - due 2011	Yes	Yes	Yes
Feature/Function	Yes	No	No	No
Feature/Function	No - due 2011	Yes	Yes	Yes

WARNING: Be prepared for customers to suggest features and/or functionality that are missing in your solutions. Include this data in your table also.

BIGGER WARNING: Do NOT focus too much on competitors. Your success primarily depends on how well you achieve key objectives rather than what your competitors are doing. Think of your work as a sport. Today in world sporting competitions often the difference between the 1st and 2nd place winners is only hundredths of a second. It is the same in business.

Achievable ideas need to be prioritized and implemented. When you communicate this to your customers, they gain emotional ownership in your product line and become advocates for you. Inappropriate or unreasonable suggestions also deserve an answer. Always explain your reasoning to the customer or employee in a polite and empathetic manner.

Keep in mind part of **your job as a manager is to understand the results, not just quote them**. Customer suggestions may not be the best solution or what they really need.

Think of it this way. When you play sports, your team loses games. Part of the coach's job is to understand WHY you lost. The coach may ask the players and others for their opinion, but a good coach is responsible for analyzing what actions on the field created specific results, and then determining what needs to be changed to increase the potential to win.

Think beyond the answers you receive from customers and your people as to why they are struggling to use your products. Often it is as simple as they do not believe the benefit of using your products outweighs the initial loss of time it takes to learn how to properly use your solutions.

Most of the time customers are clueless about how to innovate products and often provide feedback simply based on competitor product features. Never forget: The responsibility of determining your next bold move in business is yours, not your customers'.

Studying the competition and knowing facts about your own solutions by itself is not enough. You need to motivate your employees to practice *LOI: Live It – Observe It – Improve It.*

Live It

Live It means whatever product or service you sell, you must regularly use it yourself. If you sell bicycles, then buy one and ride it. If you sell soap, then wash with it. Stocks, then invest your money in stocks. Software, then use it yourself.

What if you sell airplanes? If you do, then at least ride in one of your company manufactured planes often enough to understand what your clients and their customers experience when riding in your aircraft. Talk to pilots, mechanics, flight attendants, and baggage handlers to learn what they think of your airplanes. There is always something to learn.

Some quick thoughts on how to get your people to *Live It:*

- ❏ Train your people upon hiring to *Live It*. Incorporate product training into your basic, mandatory employee-training program to motivate your people to use your products and services.

- ❏ Give each employee a single copy of your product(s) for free or at a deep discount to get it into their possession.

- ❏ Motivate your employees to use your products and services. Only by using your solutions will your employees fully comprehend why your solutions are better than competitive alternatives.

- ❏ Train constantly, not just as a one-time event. Repetition increases knowledge and expands skills. Create an ongoing learning environment that shares the best ways to use your products.

This goes back to *Understand How You Make a Difference*. Similar to your values statement, you have to *"walk the walk, not just talk the talk."* Zig Ziglar (www.ZigZiglar.com) says, *"If you're selling Chevys, you better not be driving a Mercedes."* If you make excuses for using your solutions, then you cannot be fully effective at convincing prospective customers to buy them.[33]

Author Jason Jennings, quoted in Fast Company magazine, says, *"At Sonic Drive-In, CEO Cliff Hudson insists that his executives spend at least half their time in the chain's actual kitchens – not a test kitchen at headquarters – to come up with new menu items."*[34]

Make certain your experience with your company's products and that of your employees is real.

Observe It

Not only should you *Live It*, but *Observe It* - experience your products and/or services with your customers. Three quick thoughts on why you should *Observe It:*

❑ <u>Watching your customers</u> use your products and services, or using them with your customers validates your conclusions and provides additional valuable insight into how to make your solutions the best in the world.

❑ Watching a <u>variety of your customer's employees</u> use your products gives you a totally new perspective on how to be the best.

❑ *Observe It* transforms product development from a one-time exercise into a <u>living, breathing experience</u> with you right in the middle of it with your customers.

Jason Jennings also points out that *"Jim Cabela, founder of the eponymous $1.59 billion outdoor retailing phenomenon, works until noon each day personally addressing new complaints that came in the day before."*[35]

What priority are your customers' comments? Not just to you, but to your people. And do you just work your way through them, or do you see them as an opportunity to engage more passionate customers and learn better how to serve them?

Again, let me remind you: Totally relying on your customers to drive your product strategy will fail. Customers are busy running their own business. Test your revolutionary concepts with customers and/or prospective customers who currently do not buy from you, but *innovation decisions remain your responsibility.*

Improve It

Maybe you have to improve your product through several stages or releases to ultimately make it awesome, but never accept anything about your solution that is less than the best it can be. *Improve It* means you go beyond observing your product or service failing:

- ❑ You figure out how to make it better
- ❑ Commit the resources to improve it
- ❑ Do whatever it takes to make it better
- ❑ Test it to make certain it is reliable and performs well
- ❑ Then release the upgraded solution.
- ❑ (Repeat this process over and over again.)

Think about it: Ultimately this is what your customers want you to be doing. To be a leader you need to be constantly improving everything within your influence.

WAIT! You think you have heard all this before. Let me be more specific. *I am not talking about incremental improvement.* **I want you to stretch for breakthrough thinking.**

For instance, let me give you an example using a national crisis facing America. Healthcare costs are a major problem for all of us. Maybe we need to think outside the box. Business Week reports that in India, a hospital named Narayana charges $1,500 for heart bypass surgery and operates on hundreds of infants a year for free. The hospital is highly profitable, has no debt, and claims a higher success rate than many U.S. hospitals.

How do they do it? Low wages help, but also citizens are willing to forgo malpractice lawsuits for lower cost care. Also the hospital changed the healthcare business model. In the U.S., the chief surgeon manages the entire patient process, from testing and diagnosis to supervising the operating room, recuperation and billing. At Narayana the process is more like an assembly line where surgeons only do surgery. People only do what they do best. This also leads to higher equipment usage which lowers equipment costs per patient. And so on.

Therefore when I say you must *Improve It*, I mean you have to:

- ❑ Take what you know from using your products

- ❑ Combine that knowledge with what you observe of people using your products

- ❑ And look for inspiration from your competitors or even companies outside your industry to develop more efficient business systems. (Remember *Systematic Power*…)

Consider the passion *LOI: Live It – Observe It – Improve It* instills in your employees! They become unstoppable in their quest to convince others your solutions are the best because they experience the benefits of your solutions first-hand and see its positive effect on customers.

How many times in the last month have you used your company products or services? *A common answer is none.*

That is why *LOI: Live It - Observe It - Improve It* is one of the *Desired Results* of the *Establish Your Foundation* suite. <u>*LOI* is foundational to your long-term success.</u>

As Nike used to say, *Just Do It.*[36] If you regularly follow a diet and exercise program, you lose weight and increase muscle tone. If you follow a proven system to manage your money more effectively, you save money and increase your assets.

The *Success With People* system is a proven 12-step program for managers and aspiring leaders that increases your ability to positively affect others.

When you understand <u>why</u> people buy your products and <u>how</u> your solutions improve their lives, you and your employees enjoy a motivating vision that fuels your desire to undertake activities that result in making the world a better place. You gain *passion - one of the most competitive weapons in business and something that makes your work personally fulfilling.*

Changing the world… now that is exciting!

Conclusion

Incorporate *LOI: Live It - Observe It - Improve It* regularly into your workday. Be consistent in *LOI* to <u>make certain your products and services are superior to your competition.</u> You can see below how our systems and commitment to develop employee passion are feeding off one another to fuel company growth.

<u>Establish Your Foundation</u>

1. *Systematic Power* is a commitment to hire, manage, develop and retain talent systematically.

2. *Understand How You Make a Difference* makes working for your company a meaningful experience and fuels employee passion to achieve.

3. *LOI: Live It - Observe It - Improve It* involves your employees with your products to increase their passion for your company and ability to serve clients better.

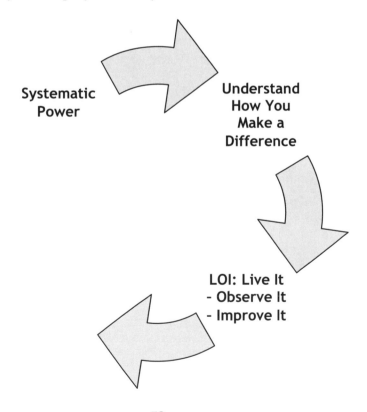

Live It - Observe It - Improve It involves your employees with your products to increase their passion for your company and ability to serve clients better. Here is a quick summary.

✓ Do an analysis of your competition (not too lengthy).

✓ Determine how many of your people actually use the products and/or services your company sells.

✓ Encourage your people to use your company products and services on a regular basis, <u>and provide feedback</u> in writing and/or presentations – both positive and negative.

✓ Train and retrain your people on how to use your products and services. Hold them accountable to do so at no cost or low cost to them.

✓ Observe customers using your products to learn how to make their experience better – *then do something about it!*

✓ Have your people regularly talk with customers, survey them, and <u>listen</u> with an open mind. Think beyond the recommendations of your people and customers to visualize and develop better customer experiences with your solutions.

✓ Test and stress your solutions to observe how they break so you can identify how to improve them.

✓ Leverage the information gained in *LOI: Live It – Observe It – Improve It* so your conclusions develop passion in your employees and better solutions for customers.

Sanctuary

Desired Result #4

Jim Loehr and Tony Schwartz wrote, *"The biggest problem in American business today is the feeling that nothing is ever finished. There is no satisfaction to be derived from a job well done because there is always another demand to be met. We are all running on an endless treadmill."*[37]

In contrast to the "endless treadmill," the final cornerstone of the *Establishing Your Foundation* suite is *Sanctuary,* which is comprised of three thoughtful activities:

❑ *Rest*

❑ *Reflection*

❑ *Risk*

For many people *Sanctuary* is a spiritual break from the world. I do not mean to cheapen the term, but rather extend it to be a pause to recover, reflect, gain strength, and focus for our careers.

Rest

Most of us need a way to recover from the hectic pace of our lives. We need to adopt a sustainable lifestyle that better balances our work and personal lives. One proven method to help achieve this is to experience *Sanctuary* every two to four hours during your workday. Studies have proven people who take breaks at work improve their effectiveness.

A Duke University neurobiologist[38] suggested getting up from your desk every hour for a change of scenery, even if you just take a brief, relaxed walk. His conclusion is unfamiliar sensory stimulation seems to increase your ability to receive and process information. It also makes you available to others and helps you consider details or activities that you are currently overlooking.

Loehr and Schwartz wrote a book about recovery, *The Power of Full Engagement – Managing Energy, Not Time, Is The Key to High Performance and Personal Renewal.*[39] Their claim is *"managing your energy is more important than managing your time."* One of the key actions they appear to prove is taking a break every two hours during your workday to drink water and have a healthy snack while doing something enjoyable, such as a short leisurely walk, removes stress and improves focus.

Breaks every 2 hours are a challenge for me, but I take breaks every 2-4 hours fairly consistently. The labor unions instituted regular breaks years ago. Unfortunately today union and non-union workers alike often abuse break time.

Let me tell you my struggle. I believe in *Sanctuary*, but I forget. Therefore I enter Tasks in Outlook reminding me at 10:00 a.m. and 3:00 p.m. to do some walking, swimming or stretching, along with having a healthy snack. I also have Tasks set for me at noon and 5:00 p.m. to pray with thanksgiving. These reminders help me incorporate *Sanctuary* regularly into each workday. *The result is I am much more focused on my key objectives.*

When managers do not explain or reinforce the value of work or the worker, employees are not motivated to balance focused, hard work with restful breaks. Without the motivation to achieve, workers go through the motions of work only to complete the job at a minimum standard rather than strive to work effectively to create awesome results

Researches at the University of Missouri did a test and proved jogging 3 times during a day for 10 minutes burns 69 percent more fat than jogging for 30 minutes at one time.[40]
(Smaller breaks taken more often are better for you.)

Taking breaks properly also *increases your ability to manage stress.* Most people do not consider stress as part of a growth cycle, but rather a symptom of stagnation in life to be endured.

A number of professional sports consultants have identified and proven an effective way to increase muscle strength is to stress the muscle beyond its normal capacity, and then allow it twenty-four to forty-eight hours to heal. This is recovery. Loehr and Schwartz have proven this system to build muscle capacity can also be leveraged in other areas of our life to build physical, emotional, mental, and spiritual abilities.

Reflect

The second part of *Sanctuary* is to *Reflect*. Reflection clears your mind of business or whatever is stressing your system. As you *Rest*, remove yourself from your stress environment. Go for a leisurely walk, drink some water, eat a healthy snack, and listen to your thoughts. Some people focus on things for which they are thankful. Others dream, many pray or meditate, and some enjoy quietly talking to themselves.

Reflecting is a good time to get a handle on your negative thoughts. It is best to never let your people hear you complain about the company, other employees, or your personal life. As a leader, if you set a standard that complaining is acceptable, then your people will follow your example.

This does NOT mean you avoid addressing problems, correcting service or product defects, or neglect to consider both the positive and negative sides of a situation. Just remember the more positive you are, the more positive your people will be.

I used this technique in my first business. I had started a trade show business. A guy named Terry who had done many shows gave me one piece of advice for when I was in the exhibit hall. He told me to always have a smile on my face and look confident, like everything was going according to plan, even if attendance was low which it was at that first show.

Show attendance was poor yet because I took breaks to gain perspective, I was not stressed out. The result was all but one exhibitor agreed the show was new and they were aware of the risks. In part because I was positive, they remained positive.

When considering negative situations, consider the following:

1. Everyone is doing their best. If someone's behavior is not up to your standards, you basically have 2 options: Train the person better or start a process to let him go.

2. Be thankful for the good things the person has done. Remind yourself of what the person is doing right. It may turn out this inspires you to understand her core competencies (natural talent) really is.

    You may decide the person is not the problem, but she is in the wrong job. She may actually be awesome in another position. Assessments can provide valuable insights to help with this decision (see *Right Person – Right Job, Desired Result #7*).

3. If part of the problem is you made a mistake, then learn from it and move on. When an employee errors then discuss it with him, explain how to avoid the mistake in the future, train him if necessary, document it, and move on (see *Listen More – Desired Result #9*). Forgive and forget, whether the problem was with you or someone else. *Do not let the past take your future away.*

4. Lastly, always remember life is too short. Try to dance when no one is looking *and keep laughing!*

Many people feel guilty when they pause to *Reflect* on the job. We are programmed and monitored to be "working" and we are moving so fast it feels uncomfortable to stop and just think.

Think about how many times you have moved too quickly and did not fully consider an opportunity, a co-worker's personality, or completely explore the risk of a decision prior to moving ahead. The result was confrontation, higher costs or outright failure.

The costs of not taking time to *Reflect* are too high.

If you are concerned people might misunderstand your *Sanctuary* time then have your primary *Sanctuary* alone early in the morning or late in the day. It is often the best time anyway.

Risk

The last component of *Sanctuary* is *Risk*. Use *Sanctuary* to balance your emotions when considering taking *Risks* in your life. Rushing into a *Risk* as a shortcut typically results in failure. Avoid shortcuts. Success is a process that rarely is achieved on the quickest timeframe.

Sanctuary enables you to withdraw from your constant motion and thought to *Rest*, which restores strength. As you recover, *Reflect* to gain clarity about the process involved in achieving your objectives. Then evaluate from a broader perspective the pros and cons of your *Risk* decision.

Tony Campolo once quoted a study of people over the age of 95 who were asked if they had to live their lives over again, what they would do differently. One thing mentioned was they would *Risk* more.[41]

Here are a few tips on how to evaluate *Risks*:

1. Only *Risk* what is consistent with your values. Do not take careless risks because they often hurt others. Live by the Golden Rule to treat others as you prefer to be treated.

2. Avoid rushing into *Risk*. Well thought out, reasonable *Risks* can be a good decision because often some *Risk* is necessary to achieve great accomplishments.

3. Do not take unnecessary *Risk* with O.P.M. (Other People's Money). For instance, if you want your creditors to always pay you what they owe on time then avoid a *Risk* that might eliminate your ability to pay your vendors before their bill is due.

4. Several small *Risks* are better than one big one that can sink you.

5. Do not make *Risk* decisions alone. Involve others who are sharing the *Risk*, then leverage *Sanctuary* to identify the best decision based on facts, not emotion.

Make certain you *Rest* during the day and each week so you can recover physically, spiritually, mentally and/or emotionally. *Reflect* to gain perspective and then make *Risk* decisions carefully.

Try to **balance emotion in your decision-making** process when considering a *Risk*. Do not compromise your integrity for a temporary financial gain or the attention you may receive.

Years ago a high tech executive was winning a prize for being the Entrepreneur of The Year. His company was not the largest or by some standards the best, but it was highly respected and this executive was often quoted in the press.

As part of his acceptance speech this executive proudly showed a picture of his large 40-person executive team and praised them for how hard they worked. He went on to boast his team was so committed to his company that none were still married to their first spouse. His point was work was more important than family.

Unfortunately this man and his team took the wrong *Risk*. Learn from their mistake.

This is why leveraging proven methods of managing people must include a balance with personal *Sanctuary*. Make certain you get *Rest*, take time to *Reflect*, and take a *Risk* only when it is consistent with your values.

The basics of life are relatively simple. *People make life difficult with bad choices.* Someone once said to me, *"You don't always get what you want, but you always get what you choose."* Be disciplined enough in your life to maintain a balance.

Many years ago I was between jobs and went to work for a friend. Although he was very successful, it was a *Risk* because of the potential personality clash between us. My friend and I put aside our concerns because others were encouraging us to work together.

After 3 weeks I realized he did not want me to work there any longer. When I offered to leave, he agreed. In that meeting I asked if it would be okay for me to continue to work in his industry, but not compete with him. He agreed. The next day we exchanged some artwork and the business relationship ended.

A day or two later he changed his mind. He did not want me to work in his industry. I had very convincing reasons as to why it was reasonable for me to continue to work in his industry and I did so without competing with him. Nevertheless as a result of our decisions, the friendship ended.

Years later I realized my decision was wrong. If I had practiced *Sanctuary* in my life, I would have been balanced enough to understand the following:

1. The *Risk* to our friendship was too high to accept the job, particularly because my natural interests did not align with his industry. The work was not meaningful for me. I was just being lazy about finding a more appropriate job.

2. When it came time to leave the job, I would have had faith there were other career opportunities to pursue. I was not limited to staying in his industry.

3. It would have been clear the most important objective was to maintain our friendship, even if his request seemed unreasonable. After briefly working for him, I should have left his industry and just found other work.

You may have so much going on at work it seems taking *Sanctuary* is impossible. You are wrong. It is challenging and takes discipline, but you can do it.

One way to free up some time: Say "no" the next time someone asks you to do something that does not absolutely have to be done (by you) – more on this in *Success Plans* (*Desired Result #5*).

Conclusion

The fourth cornerstone of the *Success With People* system is *Sanctuary*. You need to give yourself recovery time to sustain excellent performance, <u>but most importantly you need time to pause and reflect on the decisions you are making</u>. You also need to train your people to use *Sanctuary* for improved performance and results.

Now you have the four *Desired Results* cornerstones of the *Establish Your Foundation* suite:

<u>Establish Your Foundation</u>

1. *Systematic Power* is a commitment to hire, manage, develop and retain talent systematically.

2. *Understand How You Make a Difference* makes working for your company a meaningful experience and fuels employee passion to achieve.

3. *Live It - Observe It - Improve It* involves your employees with your products to increase their passion for your company and ability to serve clients better.

4. *Sanctuary* combines *Rest, Reflect,* and *Risk* to give you a clearer perspective, renewed energy and inspirational creativity to achieve your best.

These are foundational because

❑ Systems provide the basis to repeat and scale best practices.

❑ Meaningful work increases productivity, personal fulfillment and employee retention. It is also established and maintained by your systems.

❑ *LOI* gets everyone involved in your products, adding to the meaning in their work and improving your solutions.

❑ *Sanctuary* provides valuable perspective, which in turn impacts LOI, increases the meaning in your work and improves your systems.

This is your foundation for superior talent management, but notice <u>it is fluid</u> rather than stationary. Keep working these *Desired Results* regularly in your business to fully develop employee passion and meaningful, profitable work.

**Systematic
Power**

**Understand
How You
Make a
Difference**

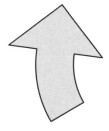

Sanctuary

**LOI: Live It
- Observe It
- Improve It**

Sanctuary combines *Rest, Reflect,* and *Risk* to give you a clearer perspective, renewed energy and inspirational creativity to achieve your best. Here is a quick summary.

✓ Rest by taking breaks every 2-4 hours when working – remove yourself from your stress zone to leisurely walk, stretch, snack on something healthy, and reflect.

✓ Reflect by praying, meditating, pausing and/or listening to your thoughts. Let your mind wander to consider life beyond work or at the very least, possible solutions between two extremes with which you are struggling.

✓ Risk only when it is consistent with your personal values. Slow down and reflect more. If you feel you have to rush into something – *quick decisions are often a sign you are avoiding staying true to your values*.

✓ Lastly, let me remind you: The most important attribute of *Sanctuary* is to *Reflect*. This is a time to hear inspiration for new solutions and consider the true outcomes of your decisions.

Balance Your Workload

Success
Plans

Pass The Baton
on Job
Responsibilities

Compensation
That Pays

Right
Person
Right Job

Success Plans

Desired Result #5

Next is the *Balance Your Workload* suite of the *Success With People* system. The first of these *Desired Results* helps you control the events of your day so you become a better steward of your time and resources. I call this tool, *Success Plans*.

After over two decades of struggling to balance my priorities, I studied different systems for managing my time more effectively. Today Franklin Covey, DayRunner, Microsoft and lots of other companies offer tools to organize your life. All of these solutions lacked something or took too much time for me. That is why I developed my *Success Plans*.

Here is a story to help make my point. I am not aware of its origination although I have been emailed it a few times. I have changed the story slightly.

A professor stood before his philosophy class and had some items in front of him. When the class began, wordlessly, he picked up a very large and empty mayonnaise jar and proceeded to fill it with golf balls. He then asked the students if the jar was full. They agreed that it was.

The professor then picked up a box of pebbles and poured them into the jar. He shook the jar lightly. The pebbles cascaded into the open areas between the golf balls. He repeated the process. He then asked the students again if the jar was full. They agreed that it was.

The professor next picked up a box of sand and poured it into the jar. He shook the jar lightly to help the sand filter into the open areas of the jar. He repeated the process. He asked the class once more if the jar was full. The students responded with a unanimous, "Yes!"

The professor then produced two cups of tea from under the table and poured the entire contents into the jar, effectively filling the empty space between the sand. The students laughed.

"Now," said the professor as the laughter subsided, "I want you to recognize this jar represents your life.

"The golf balls are the important things in life - your relationship with God, family, your children, your health, your friends, and your favorite passions -- things that if everything else was lost and only they remained, your life would still be fulfilling.

"The pebbles are material things such as your job, house, and car.

"The sand is everything else -- the small stuff.

"If you put the pebbles or the sand into the jar first," he continued, "there is no room for the golf balls. The same goes for life. If you spend all your time and energy on material things and the small stuff, you never have room for the people or activities that are truly important to you.

"Make certain you invest your time in people and activities that are meaningful and critical to your happiness. Play with your children. Enjoy exercising. Take your spouse and special others out for fun. Marvel at nature. Meet with friends. There will always be time to clean the house and do more work.

"Always take care of the golf balls first -- the things that really matter. <u>Set your priorities and live by them</u>. The rest of life is just sand."

One of the students raised her hand and inquired what the tea represented.

The professor smiled. "I'm glad you asked. It's to show you that no matter how full your life may seem, there's always room for a couple of cups of tea and conversation with a friend."

Hyrum Smith, the founder of Franklin-Covey and The Galileo Initiative (www.GalileoInitiative.com) teaches *"To gain control of our lives, we must gain control of our time."* This is good counsel.

You may still use your calendar for appointments and software to remind you of tasks. The priorities you set in your *Success Plans* enable you to control the push and pull of unexpected events rather than replace your existing time management solution.

Achieving key priorities is crucial to enjoying *Success With People*. Here is how I do it.

❑ A weekly *Success Plan*, focused primarily on personal goals, and

❑ Daily *Success Plans* (workdays) focused on business goals

General Layout

Create your *Success Plan* form with pictures of something important to you across the top. It might be pictures of a family vacation, friends, heroes, gifts, comics, dreams or anything to make you smile and be motivated during the upcoming week. (See samples pages 73-74 which can be downloaded from our website, or create your own.)

Top Ten: Title and date your *Success Plan*. On the right side below the date, maintain a list of your *Top Ten* initiatives, which are the priorities you are pursuing during the current year. Circle the number next to the Top Ten goal whenever you do something that moves you closer to achieving it. **This regular interaction with your *Top Ten* is important.**

You may have some *Top Ten* items that are never completed, such as the first on my weekly *Success Plan*, which is my prayer time. This is an ongoing priority during the year. It is also a *Top Ten* objective because it affects my personal and professional life.

Maintain the *Top Ten* list to focus on achieving personal and professional initiatives each year. It can be more effective to have less than 10 key objectives. Life is overflowing with choices. The key is to keep your *Top Ten* list simple, focused and balanced.

Balanced means if 80 percent of the items on your *Top Ten* list are all business activities, then your focus is not balanced between your personal and professional lives. Prioritize your *Top Ten* without considering whether a goal is personal or professional.

There are two determining factors that enable you to achieve balance in your life most of the time. You must be willing to:

1. Spend less than you earn.

2. Say, "No." (You can<u>not</u> do everything.)

** **Your *Top Ten* must be specific**, or it will not be accomplished. Do not say, *"Read books."* Write, *"Read two books a month."*

Personal Development: Below your *Top Ten* consider having one personal development goal. This reminds you to work on a key area needing improvement or get even stronger in an area where you have natural ability. Check it off or circle it each day or week that you work on it.

Do It Now and Other Achievements: Many experts recommend you list your objectives and then divide them into two groups. Some call this an "A" and a "B" list.

Instead I suggest the first group be named a *Do It Now* list indicating goals that <u>absolutely must be achieved</u> today or this week, depending on the *Success Plan*. Objectives you would like to accomplish, but are not totally necessary go on your *Other Achievements* list. Each list is written in priority so you focus on #1 first, then #2 and so on.

Other experts teach you to maintain a "C List" for non-critical objectives. *My experience is the C List has no value.* If you identify something you want to accomplish yet it is only a "C" priority then do one of three things.

- Cross it off the list and forget about it. Usually it is just not important enough to take the place of your other priorities and not worth your time to track for the future.

- Recognize the objective is tied to another project, but it is not necessary to achieve until sometime in the future. Then add the objective to a list or folder you have for that project. If necessary enter a task in software with an alarm to remind you when to reconsider the objective.

- Accept the fact the item is not an objective, but an idea. In that case write it down and date it, then place it in a file for future reference. If it is online, then save the page to a folder containing those type of ideas. You can have files with book ideas, movie ideas, vacation ideas, your plans how to change the world or remodel your bathroom!

Do NOT let your daydreaming distract you from achieving your priorities.

Commit yourself to achieving your *Do It Now* list in the order you have listed them – from most important (#1) to least important. The only exception is when you make a conscious decision to replace it with another activity that has become more important.

Do It Now objectives are specific. An example of a *Do It Now* objective is, *"Complete the widget project proposal"* or *"Practice PPT presentation for 30 minutes."*

Check-off each *Do It Now* objective as you achieve it. I circle the number next to a *Do It Now* objective if my work is completed and the item requires a response from someone else to be complete.

Weekly Success Plan

Weekly Success Plans are optional. For many people a *Daily Success Plan* is all that is needed. Start your week sometime on Sunday in a place removed from all distractions. Write your *Success Plan* for the upcoming week during this *Sanctuary* time

First review your prior week's *Success Plan* to understand what you achieved. Take a moment to reflect on those accomplishments. Any remaining objectives must be considered for the upcoming week. Glance at email and planned tasks for the upcoming week only to remind you of responsibilities, not to respond to them.

Assign 1-3 *Do It Now* objectives to each day. Make it a minimum of what you must accomplish that day. Do NOT list extra items that just carry forward like a "to do list." This is NOT a "to do list," but a commitment to accomplish specific goals each day.

A Weekly *Success Plan* focuses your efforts on a limited number of objectives each day in contrast to writing a long list of tasks to achieve for the week. The long list is often overwhelming and adds stress. It may tempt you subconsciously not to work on your tasks until midweek and then all your tasks do not get completed.

As you prepare mentally to write your *Success Plan*, consider:

❑ *Reflect*ing on my *Top Ten* and whether my activities are helping me achieve these key objectives.

❑ What needs to be achieved from last week's *Success Plan*?

❑ Tasks I am tracking in Outlook or other software.

❑ What can I delegate to others?

❑ What do I need to follow-up on that was delegated?

Daily Success Plan

Limit the majority of your daily plan to business objectives. Another area I have added to my *Daily Success Plan* is *This Week's Plan*. In this box I list a maximum of 3 key objectives for the week. The purpose of having this on my daily plan is so each day I am checking myself against these objectives daily or possibly I am not writing a *Weekly Success Plan* this week.

The beauty of *Success Plans* is they are totally flexible. The *Do It Now*, *Other Achievements* and *Top Ten* are the core essentials, but you can design them any way you want. Samples of basic weekly and daily *Success Plans* are on the next two pages.

Dave's Success Plan for May 24-30, 2010

Do It Now

Monday: Red rose for Bear

Meet with Leukemia Society

Tuesday: Prepare for presentation

Touch base with apprentices on Success Plan progress

Wednesday: Complete review of Business Plan

Thursday: Write Chapter 8

Practice Chamber of Commerce presentation

Friday: Touch base with apprentices on Success Plan progress

Saturday: Build another raised garden (call James)

Sunday: Hike

Email/mail draft for comments

Other Achievements

Rotate car tires

Get photos developed

Top Ten

1. Bible study and prayer daily
2. Complete tasks and reminders daily
3. Balance work, family, x work, exercise
4. Weekly track goal progress by manager
5. Romantic act for Terry each week
6. Develop new training program by 6/30
7. Fellowship time weekly
8. Monthly work for Leukemia Society

Objective Judgment

- Structure decision-making process
- Seek info from more sources

73

Dave's Success Plan for May 24, 2010

Do It Now

Personal

1. Permit to cut tree down
2. Teacher conference with Bob

Business

1. Complete/reschedule all calls/reminders
2. Write editorial for Daily News
3. Plan 3rd Quarter marketing campaign for Roy

Other Achievements

Personal

1. New tires for van

Business

1. Letter for Small Business Bundle
2. Email consultants – story from Ruth about coaching client
3. Set-up dual database for work
4. Schedule account reviews

Top Ten

1. Bible study and prayer daily
2. Complete tasks and reminders daily
3. Balance work, family, x work, exercise
4. Weekly track goal progress by manager
5. Romantic act for Terry each week
6. Develop new training program by 6/30
7. Fellowship time weekly
8. Monthly help for Leukemia Society

This Week's Plan

1. Practice speech daily
2. Finish new web site

Objective Judgment

- Structure decision-making process
- Seek info from more sources

If you structure your daily *Do It Now* list properly, you often can achieve some objectives on the *Other Achievements* list each day.

Handwrite completed any accomplishment on your *Success Plan* that is not on either list, but you decided to achieve it rather than an activity on your *Do It Now* and *Other Accomplishments* lists.

One major reason people lives are out of balance is because we want *"to have it all."* Humans are not designed that way. Stop believing the advertising that says you <u>need</u> it all. Your needs are quite different from your wants. Life is fulfilling when we achieve our priorities rather than pursuing every whim.

Years ago Marc Andresson, a Netscape founder, was asked the greatest benefit of selling his company. He said he enjoyed a full night's sleep and as a result, his thoughts were clearer and he was more productive.

What a blessing it is for our lives to be overflowing with options! This opportunistic freedom attracts thousands of immigrants to America every year to escape the oppression of their home nation.

Yet we must always remember freedom requires responsibility, and true success in life cannot be achieved without balance.

Brian G. Dyson, when he was President and CEO of Coca-Cola Enterprises, spoke at the Georgia Tech 172nd Commencement. One key point he made about balance in your life was this:

"Imagine life as a game in which you are juggling some five balls in the air. You name them – work, family, health, friends and spirit – and you're keeping all of these in the air. You will soon understand that work is a rubber ball. If you drop it, it will bounce back. But the other four balls – family, health, friend and spirit – are made of glass. If you drop one of these, they will be irrevocably scuffed, marked, nicked, damaged or even shattered. They will never be the same. You must understand that and strive for balance in your life."[A2]

This is one reason the different Desired Results build upon one another for maximum effectiveness and balance.

For instance, the *Top Ten* list of your *Success Plan* helps you maintain balance between your daily/weekly objectives, and keep you focused on true priorities rather than seemingly urgent tasks. *Sanctuary* provides the opportunity to *Rest, Reflect* and a renewed perspective on *Risk*. Other *Desired Results* help focus you on achieving goals through others.

Each day has specific priorities and choices. This is why you write a daily version of your *Success Plan* each morning or before you leave the office each evening for the following day.

One last analogy: Think of balance in life as a clock pendulum. It swings from side-to-side to move time forward. Our personal balance is a process of moving from a lot of activity to no activities. You are out of balance if you are constantly working and/or stressed-out and you are not resting to recover. Although technically the "balance" is when the pendulum is straight up and down, in reality for most people balance is a rhythm of life between the two extremes.

Some people believe balance is impossible. For instance, Keith H. Hammonds, Deputy Editor of Fast Company magazine wrote:

"The truth is, balance is bunk. It is an unattainable pipe dream, a vain artifice that offers mostly rhetorical solutions to problems of logistics and economics. The quest for balance between work and life, as we've come to think of it, isn't just a losing proposition; it's a hurtful, destructive one." [43]

I totally disagree (and many readers did also).

Balance in life is not "bunk," it is a choice many people are unwilling to embrace.

Here are two disciplined behaviors to help you achieve balance through your *Success Plans*.

❑ Limit objectives on your *Do It Now* list. <u>Results are what count.</u> Be disciplined, not overly optimistic. It is better to be wildly successful in one focused activity than average in many. Limit yourself to 1-3 *Do It Now* items daily.

❑ Get started on your *Do It Now* list immediately each morning and try to complete those objectives as early in the day or week as possible. This way you have enough time to do really great work in achieving your priorities, and may have time left over for other opportunities.

What if you do items 1 and 2 on your *Do It Now* list, and then skip to #5 on your *Other Achievements* list? Sometimes that happens. Possibly something occurred to convince you another objective is more important. This is okay as long as you <u>make a conscious decision</u> to change your priorities and it is not a daily practice.

Realize however, disciplining yourself to achieve the list in the order written saves time, lowers stress and better develops long-term success. If you are uncertain you can do this because people constantly come to you with emergencies that need immediate attention, then the key is to make a choice about your priorities.

Allocate your time based on one of two criteria:

❑ The importance of the task relative to your other objectives, and

❑ Urgent situations, such as a deadline about to be missed or an employee has an emergency requiring your attention.

If you choose to react to what seems to be a priority, but is not on your *Success Plan*, you end up racing around yet ending each day feeling you achieved nothing of importance. One day you wake up to find you are out of shape physically, emotionally out of touch with your closest friends, spiritually disconnected, and not delivering your best results at work.

When an urgent task comes up that seems to require your time immediately, you have two options:

❑ Compare the urgency of the request to your *Do It Now* list. If the request is not more important than your *Do It Now* items, then try to say no. Simply apologize, say you cannot do what is being requested and explain your other priorities that must be done.

❑ Explain your objectives for today to the person with the urgent task. Ask that person which of your priorities should be set aside so you can do his urgent task. Do this politely and with sincere empathy for his request. *Do not be rude.* (This type of response is very effective with bosses that give their employees too much to do.)

There are three situations where this does not work.

- You raise a concern about being overloaded but you are often on personal calls or having personal conversation in the office. In this case your *personal* activities are eliminating work time. Please understand personal phone calls, emails, conversation, errands, and bathroom breaks are not part of work time. Those activities are to be completed during break time or outside of work hours.

- If you are rude to the person asking you to help, this creates a problem. For instance, maybe you are stressed-out and you forgot basic manners and respect. If this happens, apologize quickly and sincerely.

- You are not willing to change your priorities. Maybe you need to reconsider and rearrange your priorities for the day. The key is to make a conscious choice to do so rather than just allow others to interrupt your progress. If you truly believe this new urgent task is more important than something else you had planned for the day, then change your priorities. If not, then stay focused on your key objectives.

Success Plans might sound like a lot of work, but actually it is quite easy as long as you keep your objectives brief. You must have a set of plans to build a house. Your *Success Plans* provide a blueprint for you to build your day around results-oriented activities rather than random behavior.

Your *Top Ten* list defines the major objectives you want to achieve this year. Your *Do It Now* and *Other Achievements* lists define key actions / priorities that lead to achieving your *Top Ten* list.

Take the challenge to simplify your life on a daily basis. Writing a daily *Success Plan* takes about 5-10 minutes each day, but it gives you tremendous focus. It saves you much more than 10 minutes daily in your improved ability to focus on key objectives. It also feels good when you check something off you accomplished.

I suggest you view most phone calls and following-up with customers as "activities" rather than priorities for a *Do It Now* or *Other Achievements* list. Be reminded to do activities in your planner or calendar software. Typically my first *Do It Now* objective is to complete my daily tasks and reminders.

Review your weekly personal *Success Plan* each day to track your progress. The combination of a daily and weekly *Success Plan* keeps your life simple. <u>Limit each *Success Plan* to one side of a single 8.5 x 11" piece of paper</u>. The activities that absolutely have to get done should be on your daily *Success Plan*. The others can be entered as reminders somewhere.

Teach your managers and employees to write *Success Plan*s and hold them accountable to do so. This is a simple way to help your people focus on key objectives. It also helps them to achieve a greater balance in their lives so they are working as efficiently and effectively as possible.

The way to get your managers and employees to leverage *Success Plans* is set the example by doing *Success Plans* yourself. Then use Log Events to remind yourself to ask to see their *Success Plans* and compliment them on doing them. (More on Log Events in *Listen More* (*Desired Result #9*).

The other reason to train your employees and have their managers hold them accountable to *Success Plan*s is to train up your next generation of managers. At the very least hold them accountable for writing and implementing a weekly <u>business</u> *Success Plan*.

WARNING: Make certain you fully comprehend the complete time commitment of each item listed on your *Do It Now* list. For instance, you may want to sign-up to mentor someone.

Signing-up is easy, but the time each week to mentor or coach is probably significant. Make certain you *Reflect* on the entire commitment first.

Do you remember *Sanctuary*? *Reflect* while writing your *Success Plan* to make the best choices for your time during the upcoming day or week. This time is actually very energizing. It helps you identify key objectives and gain confidence they can be achieved for a very fulfilling week.

Are you addicted to your "to do lists" and want to continue using them? You still can, just limit your "to do list" to activities or tasks that help you achieve your *Do It Now* or *Top Ten* lists.

Conclusion

General Electric CEO, Jeff Immelt, once said,

"There is no real magic to being a good leader. But at the end of every week, <u>you have to spend your time around the things that are really important</u>: setting priorities, measuring outcomes, and rewarding them."[44]

Your company may not be the size of GE, but the importance and benefits of achieving priorities are the same. As my friend, Joe, says, *"Work is the process of creating order out of chaos."* Your *Success Plan* does help. Let me give you 3 final tips:

❑ Avoid doing personal activities during your work time. When you work – <u>work</u>!
❑ No one dies regretting they did not finish a proposal for their boss. Balance work, *Sanctuary* and personal time.

❑ If writing your *Do It Now* list is stressful for you, then there are too many items listed. Identify true priorities in *Sanctuary*.

Here is what you have learned so far:

Establish Your Foundation

1. *Systematic Power* is a commitment to hire, manage, develop and retain talent systematically.

2. *Understand How You Make a Difference* makes working for your company a meaningful experience and fuels employee passion to achieve.

3. *LOI: Live It - Observe It - Improve It* involves your employees with your products to increase their passion for your company and ability to serve clients better.

4. *Sanctuary* combines *Rest, Reflect,* and *Risk* to give you a clearer perspective, renewed energy and inspirational creativity to achieve your best.

Balance Your Workload

5. *Success Plans* help you achieve key goals by balancing personal and professional objectives more effectively.

Success Plans are the first step to *Balancing Your Workload.* Check out samples on our website. By the way, certainly someone can create a *Success Plan* that is more graphically appealing than my versions. If you are so inclined, please email me a copy so it can be posted it for others to consider.

Success Plans

Success Plans, help you achieve key goals by balancing personal and professional objectives more effectively. Here is a quick summary

✓ Use daily/weekly *Success Plans* to help balance business and personal objectives while still achieving key goals. (See samples on page 73-74 or download free samples from our web site.)

✓ Use pictures on your *Success Plans* to remind you of important people, goals, and dreams in your life.

✓ Maintain a *Top Ten* list (a maximum of 10, but can be less) of your priorities for this year.

✓ Keep your *Top Ten* list balanced between personal and professional goals.

✓ Limit *Do It Now* objectives to 1-3 in a day, prioritized in order of importance, and work the items in sequence.

✓ Maintain your list of *Other Achievements* in priority.

✓ Make certain your *Do It Now* and *Other Achievements* are necessary steps to achieving your *Top Ten*.

✓ Limit your *Success Plans* to one side of a single piece of paper.

✓ If necessary to postpone a *Do It Now* objective, do so consciously.

Pass The Baton on Job Responsibilities

Does your company use job descriptions to define the responsibilities of each employee?

Too many companies have job titles, but nothing written down as a formal job description. If something is written down, it is minimal. The belief is everyone knows what to do.

Here are common problems with job descriptions. See if any of these apply to your company. Your job descriptions are:

- ❑ Non-existent

- ❑ Limited to the job title and a short list of responsibilities

- ❑ Without competencies (desired behaviors) necessary to perform the work well

- ❑ Without specific qualifications, skills, or other requirements

- ❑ Lacking specifics about the physical demands of the job and/or your work environment (not compliant with the Americans with Disabilities Act)

- ❑ Written in different formats by different people

- ❑ Not current with today's responsibilities of the position(s)

- ❑ Sitting in a file drawer and never looked at together by the manager and employee

The reason to discuss job descriptions *before* your hiring process is prior to offering anyone a job, you must define the responsibilities of the job. The purpose of a "job description" is to transfer responsibilities to an employee – that is why I call it, *Pass The Baton on Job Responsibilities*, not just *give someone a job*.

Once the person is hired or transferred to a position, the job description needs to be reviewed with the new employee. It is VERY important the employee understands everything in the job description and agrees to every responsibility.

At the end of the meeting to *Pass The Baton*, both manager and employee should sign two copies of the job description confirming the employee is committed to fulfill those responsibilities and the manager is dedicated to supporting the employee. Both retain a copy to remind them of their obligation. The manager places the signed original in the employee's file, and makes a copy or attaches a digital copy to the employee's profile in performance management software for later review.

A balanced approach means job descriptions should be reviewed by manager and employee annually at a minimum and quarterly at a maximum. Often no changes are necessary. Although the manager schedules this meeting with the employee, the employee should lead the job description review meeting. The employee should state based on her experience what changes should be made to the job description and confirm areas to remain the same.

This is important because when the employee makes the changes she takes more ownership for the results. Because you *Pass The Baton on Job Responsibilities* when the employee accepted the position, the employee owns the job and has the responsibility to update it. Start with the employee's suggestions, recommend your changes, and then agree upon the final version.

You may find some of your employees taking on too much responsibility. *Be careful to help them accept only duties they can reasonably achieve.*

Job description review meetings help employees stay on track, focus on key responsibilities, and remind managers of the specific responsibilities of their people. The review meetings are energizing for employees. How often you have these meetings is up to you and may vary per employee.

To save time writing job descriptions, you can use software. Visit our web site for our most current recommendation. Using software also helps you write all your job descriptions in a consistent format.

Remember a policy manual establishes rules for how people work, but that is different from what they do. Your policy manual is often the first item subpoenaed in an employee lawsuit. If a question arises about the job responsibilities, then expect the job description to be requested also.

To demonstrate an employee's claim is without cause, you need well-written policies and job descriptions. This is also an issue during hiring.

For instance, a friend of mine runs a messenger-courier business. She had a man without legs apply for a courier position with the company. Although he had no legs, the man was still being considered for a job after the first interview. The man called her to say he just wanted to be turned down so he could continue to earn his unemployment benefits. My friend politely declined to do that, saying it was against the law to falsely disqualify him without completing the interview process. The man did not like my friend's answer and sued her company.

The man had no case. My friend's attorney gave the man's lawyer a copy of their company policies and job description, which included the requirements for the work environment and physical demands. After reviewing the documentation, the opposing attorney dropped the case.

The average award in an employee lawsuit today is about $300,000-500,000.[45] *In some states it is less expensive to just settle a claim for $10,000 than fight it.*

It is hard to manage your business when you are innocent and still have to pay money to defend your company from a frivolous lawsuit. For this reason some companies are purchasing employment practices liability insurance ("EPLI") to protect themselves. EPLI is not for every company. Ask your business insurance agent for information.

It used to take me one or two hours to write a good job description. Using software you can write a comprehensive job description in 15-30 minutes. The process is particularly quick and easy once the job responsibilities are clearly defined and agreed to with the employee.

You can also save time by establishing a format for your job descriptions and then <u>have your employees write the first draft</u> on their own. Encourage them to observe co-workers doing similar jobs and discuss their draft job description with co-workers. Basically they are being asked to complete a job analysis for their role in the company.

There are several benefits to this approach:

❑ The employee takes more ownership for responsibilities because she wrote them.

❑ Having the employee write the first draft of her job description saves you a lot of time.

❑ The employee who has been doing this job for awhile might actually write some responsibilities you overlooked.

❑ Co-workers help define the job responsibilities of the individual so she receives the support necessary to succeed.

Now take a moment to establish the format for a well-written job description. As with any document, there are different ways to write it. This format has been developed over the years and approved by lawyers and HR consultants.

All job descriptions must be written in a consistent format from person to person and department to department to establish everyone is treated ethically, fairly and to protect your company legally.

Consider using the following format or something similar for your job descriptions. This particular format has proven to be effective by hundreds of thousands of people (including me) because *Descriptions Now* software follows this format. Please add the disclaimer. It may save you from a lawsuit.

A job description to *Pass The Baton on Job Responsibilities* includes eight components:

1. Job title and to whom the person reports

2. Summary of essential job responsibilities, including the quality or quantity of work expected

3. Description of any supervisory responsibilities

4. Desired behaviors, or competencies, that enable the person to succeed on the job

5. Knowledge, skills and/or qualifications

6. Physical demands of the position

7. Description of the work environment

8. Explanation or disclaimer of how your company will work with prospective employees

A sample job description written in *Descriptions Now* software with our disclaimer starts on the next page. Visit our web site to download a free copy of this sample document.

Success With People
Office Manager
Job Description[46]

Job Title: Office Manager
Department: Administration
Reports To: David Russell
FLSA Status: Exempt
Prepared By: David Russell
Prepared Date: August 29, 2010
Approved By: David Russell and Employee
Approved Date: September 2, 2010

SUMMARY
Manages a variety of general office activities by performing the following duties personally or through subordinate supervisors.

ESSENTIAL DUTIES AND RESPONSIBILITIES

- Analyzes and organizes office operations and procedures such as bookkeeping, preparation of payrolls, personnel, information management, filing systems, requisition of supplies, and other clerical services.

- Maximizes office productivity through proficient use of appropriate software applications.

- Researches and develops resources that create timely and efficient workflow.

- Establishes and updates bi-annually uniform correspondence procedures and style practices.

- Formulates procedures for systematic retention, protection, retrieval, transfer, and disposal of records.

- Plans office layout, develops office budget, and initiates cost reduction programs.

- Reviews clerical and personnel records to ensure completeness, accuracy, and timeliness.

- Prepares activities reports for guidance of management.

- Coordinates activities of various clerical departments or workers within department.

- Maintains contact with customers and outside vendors.

SUPERVISORY RESPONSIBILITIES

Directly supervises three employees in the Administration department. Carries out supervisory responsibilities in accordance with the organization's policies and applicable laws.

Responsibilities include interviewing, hiring, and training employees; planning, assigning, and directing work; appraising performance; rewarding and disciplining employees; addressing complaints and resolving problems.

COMPETENCIES
To perform the job successfully, an individual should demonstrate the following competencies:

Interpersonal Skills - Focuses on solving conflict, not blaming; Maintains confidentiality; Listens to others without interrupting; Keeps emotions under control; Remains open to others' ideas and tries new things.

Delegation - Delegates work assignments; Matches the responsibility to the person; Gives authority to work independently; Sets expectations and monitors delegated activities; Provides recognition for results.

Managing People - Takes responsibility for subordinates' activities; Makes self available to staff; Provides regular performance feedback; Develops subordinates' skills and encourages growth; Fosters quality focus in others; Improves processes, products and services; Continually works to improve supervisory skills.

Ethics - Treats people with respect; Keeps commitments; Inspires the trust of others; Works with integrity and ethically; Upholds organizational values.

Organizational Support - Follows policies and procedures; Completes administrative tasks correctly and on time; Supports organization's goals and values; Supports affirmative action and respects diversity.

Professionalism - Approaches others in a tactful manner; Reacts well under pressure; Treats others with respect and consideration regardless of their status or position; Accepts responsibility for own actions; Follows through on commitments.

Attendance/Punctuality - Is consistently at work and on time; Ensures work responsibilities are covered when absent; Arrives at meetings and appointments on time.

Dependability - Follows instructions, responds to management direction; Takes responsibility for own actions; Keeps commitments; Commits to long hours of work when necessary to reach goals; Completes tasks on time or notifies appropriate person with an alternate plan.

QUALIFICATIONS

Education and/or Experience - Fifth year college or university program certificate; or two to four years related experience and/or training; or equivalent combination of education and experience.

Language Skills - Ability to read and interpret documents such as safety rules, operating and maintenance instructions, and procedure manuals. Ability to write routine reports and correspondence. Ability to speak effectively before groups of customers or employees of organization.

Mathematical Skills - Ability to add, subtract, multiply, and divide in all units of measure, using whole numbers, common fractions, and decimals. Ability to compute rate, ratio, and percent and to draw and interpret bar graphs.

Reasoning Ability - Ability to apply common sense understanding to carry out instructions furnished in written, oral, or diagram form. Ability to deal with problems involving several concrete variables in standardized situations.

Computer Skills - To perform this job successfully, an individual should have the ability to use Microsoft Internet Explorer, Outlook, Excel and Word software efficiently.

PHYSICAL DEMANDS

While performing the duties of this Job, the employee is regularly required to sit; use hands and fingers to handle or feel; and talk or hear. The employee is frequently required to reach with hands and arms. The employee is occasionally required to stand, walk, stoop, kneel, crouch, or crawl. The employee must occasionally lift and/or move up to 50 pounds. Specific vision abilities required by this job include close vision, color vision, depth perception and ability to adjust focus.

WORK ENVIRONMENT

While performing the duties of this Job, the employee is occasionally exposed to risk of electrical shock and vibration. The noise level in the work environment is usually moderate.

INTENT AND FUNCTION OF JOB DESCRIPTIONS

Job descriptions assist our company in making certain our hiring process is fairly administered and qualified employees are selected. We view job descriptions as essential to our performance appraisal system and related promotion, transfer, layoff, and termination decisions. Well-written and maintained job descriptions are also an integral part of our compensation system.

All job descriptions are reviewed to ensure only essential functions and basic duties have been included. Requirements, skills, and abilities included have been determined to be the minimal standards required to successfully perform the job whereas peripheral activities that are only incidentally related to each position have been excluded. In no instance, however, should the requirement, skills, and abilities be interpreted as all-inclusive.

Supervisors may assign additional appropriate activities and requirements. It is possible that requirements may be modified to reasonably accommodate disabled individuals in accordance with the Americans with Disabilities Act. At no time will accommodations be purposefully made which may pose serious health or safety risks to the employee or others, or which impose undue hardships on our company.

Job descriptions are not intended as and do not create employment contracts. Our company is an at-will employer. At any time employees can be terminated for any reason not prohibited by law.

Employee Signature	Date

Manager Signature	Date

#1 Job Title

The first item is to have a job title. The job title should clearly explain the person's responsibilities. Some companies like to have fun job titles, allowing people to call themselves the Queen of Customer Service, Operations Czar, or whatever.

The job title should not be offensive and everyone should have titles of a similar nature. *Fun titles can be confusing and do not necessarily look great on a future resume.* The responsibilities must be clear. Remember applicants use job titles and descriptions to evaluate opportunities with your company.

At the top write your company name, then the job title. Next write to whom the person reports, the department in which the position resides, and their FLSA (Federal Labor Standards Act) status, which is exempt or non-exempt.

Exempt people are managers who are expected to work whatever hours are necessary yet reasonable to get the job done. Non-exempt employees are hourly workers that must be paid overtime when their work exceeds 8 hours a day or 40 hours a week.

#2 Summary / Essential Duties & Responsibilities

The summary of the responsibilities is typically one sentence or brief paragraph. A clear definition of the essential functions of the job follows.

This is a crucial area of the job description to help the manager and each employee understand the duties and behaviors that demonstrate great work. The desired outcomes of the work should be described rather than a general description of the methods.

For example, one of the responsibilities might be, "Files documents in proper color-coded folders and places folders alphabetically based on category," rather than just "files folders."

It is a little more work, but much more effective because you have clearly defined the requirements of the job. The person must be organized, able to comprehend your file structure, and not be colorblind.

Use this area to be specific about the quantity and quality of work. Being specific also helps you avoid lawsuits.

#3 Supervisory Responsibilities

Next describe the person's supervisory responsibilities, if applicable. For instance, list the department and how many people the person is expected to supervise. Also note whether there are subordinate managers working for this person.

#4 Competencies

Include competencies in your job description. Competencies are behaviors you want demonstrated on the job, such as good judgment, customer service skills, arriving at work on time, or having strong consultative selling skills. Factors are specific attributes of the competency.

Ultimately competencies <u>and assessments</u> help you identify a "job match" with a candidate, but that's covered in *Right Person – Right Job (Desired Result #7)*. There are two steps to effectively identifying the best competencies for each job description.

❑ The first step looks at the job itself by clearly defining job accountabilities and determining the behaviors, motivators and competencies that are required for top performance through discussion with employees. This process involves gathering input from several people who know or do the job well. We seek to answer the question: *If the job could speak, what would it say is required for someone to be a top performer in this position?*

For example, research conducted across multiple industries has shown top performing sales people typically have a high influencing and dominant behavior style, plus they are motivated by time and money.

One of our clients determined through a detailed job analysis that people in their sales positions were also highly motivated by continuous learning and knowledge. Through interviews with sales people we identified this motivation traces back to the type of product being sold.

Their extensive reading about the product and discussions with experts taught them how the product helps with specific medical problems. These top-performing sales people were motivated to learn so they could converse effectively with medical practitioners. Their research helped them *Understand How You Make a Difference (Desired Result #2)* and close more sales.

❑ The second step of competency analysis is to understand the personality traits of your best performers in a specific job. Use assessments to confirm this information and include the competencies of your top people in similar roles in the job description.

Assessments are important because they help predict how the candidate's behavioral preferences align with the competencies required for success in the job. Learn more about in *Right Person – Right Job (Desired Result #7)*.

Remember when you discuss the employee's performance in the future you evaluate more than whether she achieved the goals you set together. You also review how she is behaving on the job.

The employee's behavior on the job dictates ultimately how well she performs and her ability to achieve goals. Including competencies on a job description helps drive improved performance. *A really nice person who does not deliver results is still ineffective and is costing your company money.*

The best approach is to have 6-10 competencies per job description. More can be confusing. Competencies help define key behavioral traits you want in a new employee and reinforce desired behaviors when the employee is on the job.

#5 Knowledge, Skills and/or Qualifications

This is where you list the experience you want the ideal candidate to have to qualify for the position. This includes education and/or experience, language skills, mathematical skills, reasoning ability, computer skills, certificates-licenses-registrations, other skills-abilities, and qualifications.

#6 Physical Demands

The physical demands are important. It is one of two items that makes your job description compliant with the Americans with Disabilities Act, or 'ADA' and certain OSHA laws. It also legally protect you when assigning work to new hires and existing employees.

#7 Work Environment

Make certain your people and new hires are very clear on the environmental aspects of their work setting. This is also important for compliance with the ADA and some other laws.

#8 Disclaimer

A disclaimer at the end of your job descriptions and space for the employee to sign are very important. Unfortunately we live in a society where many lawyers earn their living taking advantage of companies who make honest mistakes, such as not being clear on job responsibilities.

For this reason job descriptions are important to *Pass The Baton on Job Responsibilities*, but are also a critical element of legal defense in ADA, workers compensation and wrongful termination lawsuits. Just recently, a friend of mine told me a story about an employee who had filed a workers compensation claim against his company.

The employee hurt his back on a Saturday helping a friend move. Consider this occurred on the 1st of the month. The following Monday he began a week of training for a secondary job with the same company. As part of this job the employee was lifting 25-pound computer displays. During the entire week of training the employee never mentioned any back pain to fellow employees. He finally went to a doctor on the following Saturday, the 8th of the month, following his training week.

On Monday, the 10th of the month, he called into work stating the doctor wanted him home on bed rest for a week. The following Monday, the 17th of the month, he called in with the same doctor's excuse. At that time the employee was informed it was okay to take the time off, but he would not be paid for that week because he had used up his sick time the week before. At that point the employee stated his injury occurred at work and filed a claim for workers compensation.

Since my friend operates a business where his people *Understand How You Make a Difference*, he has many loyal employees. Several co-workers confirmed that on Monday, the 3rd of the month, this employee told them he had lost his footing while helping someone move a couch over the weekend and hurt his back. The story was also confirmed by a neighbor.

My friend and his employees invested over 100 hours plus attorney's fees to fight this employee through three long appeals. The employee's claim was denied each time. There are three key lessons here.

❑ My friend's company did not state in its job description the employee would be lifting 25-pound items as part of the job. That may not have eliminated the initial claim filing, but it would have reduced the employee's ability to support some of his claims.

- This employee told co-workers he hurt his back over the weekend yet none of them stopped him from lifting the displays or reported his personal injury to a manager. Teach your employees not to allow co-workers to work in a manner that might strain an existing physical injury. A manager should be notified prior to any potentially inappropriate work begins. Document the situation. You may decide the person cannot do that type of work.

- The biggest problem is the time and money my friend, his managers and employees wasted defending the case. **100 hours of lost time and attorney fees hit your profits hard.** He needed to update his job descriptions, and add employee assessments discussed in *Right Person - Right Job* (*Desired Result #7*). The assessment might have identified this person as dishonest. These three actions would have at least lowered the amount of time and money spent, if not eliminated them entirely.

Never assume your little company will always be one happy family. A lawsuit like this can really hurt you. Even for a large company, the distraction can be devastating.

Do you also see how this document clearly defines the responsibilities for the position? This attracts better applicants and you can manage people more effectively with well-written job descriptions. The fact your legal liabilities drop is an added incentive to take the time to do this right.

Your job descriptions are just one element in the *Success With People* system. The objective of the system is to help you achieve the behavioral change necessary to develop, sustain and grow a business that is mutually fulfilling for owners and employees alike.

Conclusion

As managers, your job is about replication. You want to replicate the ability of your best people and yourself to others so their work is the best it can be. This strengthens your company's ability to achieve great things.

A well-written job description sets the objectives for the job and provides the basis of a mutual understanding between manager and employee, much the same way your policies set the basic rules for engagement.

How can you avoid hiring the wrong person for the job in the first place? That is covered in the next chapter. You have now learned half of the *Success With People* system.

Establish Your Foundation

1. *Systematic Power* is a commitment to hire, manage, develop and retain talent systematically.

2. *Understand How You Make a Difference* makes working for your company a meaningful experience and fuels employee passion to achieve.

3. *LOI: Live It - Observe It - Improve It* involves your employees with your products to increase their passion for your company and ability to serve clients better.

4. *Sanctuary* combines *Rest, Reflect,* and *Risk* to give you a clearer perspective, renewed energy and inspirational creativity to achieve your best.

Balance Your Workload

5. *Success Plans* help you achieve key goals by balancing personal and professional objectives more effectively.

6. *Pass The Baton on Job Responsibilities* efficiently delegates work to your employees.

Our purpose in this suite of *Desired Results* is to *Balance Your Workload*. For leaders balancing involves delegation of work to others. Therefore first we established a process for focusing on your true key objectives each day (*Success Plans*). Part of that exercise is determining what you must do and what others can contribute as part of your team.

A well-written job description acts as a commission, a delegated influence or directive with authority for others to accomplish certain tasks on behalf of your company. Used properly, job descriptions set the stage for you to effectively *Pass The Baton on Job Responsibilities* each day and give yourself additional time to focus on what you do best.

Success Plans

Pass The Baton on Job Responsibilities

Pass The Baton on Job Responsibilities
efficiently delegates work to your employees. Here is a quick summary.

- ✓ A job description explains what an employee does – it describes the responsibilities of a job.

- ✓ If you do not have job descriptions, provide your employees with an example of the summary and key duties for a job description. Then ask your employees to write the first draft of those sections to increase their ownership of the responsibilities. (See the sample on page 88.)

- ✓ Write job descriptions in a consistent format for new positions.

- ✓ Save time and enable everyone to write job descriptions in a consistent manner by using software. Visit our web site for our most current recommendation.

- ✓ Download a sample job description including the disclaimer on our web site.

- ✓ Each employee and their manager need to agree on the job description, sign it, and retain a copy for reference.

- ✓ Managers should review each job description with their employees on a regular basis such as twice a year to affirm and encourage employees to fulfill their responsibilities or identify assistance needed.

Right Person – Right Job

Contrary to popular beliefs in general people are NOT your most important asset. Your company's two most important assets are <u>knowledge</u> combined with hiring and retaining <u>the right people</u>.

Unfortunately because some applicants write great resumes and/or give convincing interviews, and managers are in a hurry, many companies hire the wrong people and have to suffer through high employee turnover rates.

Adding stress to your hiring situation is up to 80 percent of your existing employees are actively looking for work with other companies.[47] The good news is a lot of employee turnover can be avoided.

Do the math.

> # of employees hired during the last 12 months   _____
>
> Conservative cost to replace employees   x $_____
> *(Studies estimate the cost is 50-250% of*
> *annual compensation)*
>
> Cost to replace people in the last 12 months = $_____

Here is a proven 10-step system for hiring the best and avoiding the rest. The first 3 steps involve *Establishing Your Foundation*; the next 4 steps explain *Qualifying the Candidate*; and the last 3 steps layout *Onboarding*, which is how you bring new employees into your company and get them started.

#1 – Systematic Power

Commit yourself to establishing and following a <u>system</u> for hiring. Avoid shortcuts – even candidates that seem awesome can turn out to be a nightmare if you rush your hiring process. Use this *Right Person – Right Job* hiring system or define your own and follow it.

Meet several times with your best candidate prior to extending an offer. You have known certain friends and/or your spouse for years, but how well did you know them after your first meeting? It took several meetings <u>if not years</u> to really know them. *Some of you do not even know your spouse well after 10 years of marriage!*

Why then do you expect to be able to judge a candidate accurately after only a few brief meetings when you both are working hard to make a good impression?

Right Person – Right Job means go through a complete *Success With People* process to confirm the best candidates. Once you have confirmed a candidate is a good fit based on this process, then do NOT delay. Get the employment contract signed!

#2 – Pass The Baton

Be prepared in advance with a job descriptions to *Pass The Baton on Job Responsibilities* (*Desired Result #6*). Well-written job descriptions help your hiring process in the following ways:

- ❑ Attract more qualified candidates

- ❑ Qualify people against job requirements

- ❑ Employees are clear on responsibilities

#3 – Promote The Opening

Accept the fact you are in the recruiting business. Even when you do not have openings, you need to be considering great people because long-term the quality of your employees determines your success and profitability.

Common places to find candidates include:

❏ Recruiting through your network of contacts such as

o Develop/promote from within
o Employee referrals
o Customers / vendors

❏ Online with Craigslist, Monster, CareerBuilder, … or offline in a local newspaper. Make certain you advertise the full job description or at least the web address that has it. This helps pre-qualify candidates.

❏ Long-term: Develop relationships with educational institutions in your area. High schools, junior colleges, colleges, universities and MBA programs all offer wonderful opportunities to identify fantastic employees in return for an investment of 1-2 meetings a month.

The key is to keep a pipeline of candidates active at all times just like you require your sales people to have an active pipeline of sales prospects. You want to have people available when you have a need. You want to hire quality not quantity.

Once ideal candidates are identified then begin interviewing.

Qualifying The Candidate

#4 – Interviewing

Do you realize 63% of all hiring decisions are made in the first 3 to 4 minutes of the first interview? Here is a proven interviewing process to help you identify truly super candidates.

1. **Web Search**: If the person seems like a viable candidate based on their resume and your job description, then do a web search on him on www.MSN.com, MySpace or other website. I have a friend who interviewed someone and thought he was great. When he investigated the candidate online he learned the potential hire was a white supremacist which eliminated him as a viable candidate.

Even if the person is not that bold online, some of the questions many people post answers to on their personal website include, *"In the past month have you been on drugs"* and *"In the past month have you stolen anything."* Do you want to hire someone who answers yes to either of these questions?

2. **Phone Screen**: Next schedule a time and call the person to perform a phone screen. The phone screen confirms skills listed in the resume, clarifies interest in the position, determines salary compatibility, and identifies where a candidate is in the job search process.

   The phone screen varies in length based on your objective. For sales positions the phone screen can be much more in depth because how the person sounds and responds on the phone is critical. Therefore a phone screen of a sales person may be 30-45 minutes whereas the phone screen for a technical person may be 5-15 minutes.

   Have your questions prepared in advance and remember the objective is to ask questions that get the candidate talking rather than you.

   NOTE: Many companies save time and money by asking the candidate who successfully pass a phone screen to take behavioral and motivation assessments to confirm <u>how</u> she works and <u>why</u> she works. Our *Workstyle* and *Workplace Motivators* are our two most popular online assessments. Free samples are available on our website.

   When you consider the hours your team is about to invest in interviewing a candidate, it makes sense to do this at the front-end of the process rather than later on.

3. **Interview Scorecard**: The interview scorecard is a list of behavioral-based questions for each interviewer of the candidate to ask. Write a maximum of two questions for each competency in the job description for this position.

   After interviews are complete then compare the responses – the candidate may answer differently depending on the interviewer. Save the scorecards in the candidate or employee's file to evaluate the interviews at a later date if necessary. See below for an example or visit our website to download a free sample.

INTERVIEW SCORECARD

Position: _____ Date: _____

Candidate: _____

Interviewer: _____

Other Interviewers: _____

	NOTES / RATING
Analytical Skills	Evidence of skill level: 1 2 3 4 5
Give me an example of a time when you used tools such as surveys, library research or statistics to define and solve a problem.	
Give me an example of a work flow or procedure improvement you made. Who else was involved?	
Cost Consciousness	Evidence of skill level: 1 2 3 4 5
Tell me about a time when you had to deny an expense request for budgetary reasons. How did you handle it?	
Give me an example of a time when you had to reduce expenses. How did you determine where to cut costs? What was the impact?	

Delegation	Evidence of skill level: 1 2 3 4 5
Tell me about a time you delegated a task or project to someone and met with resistance. What did you do?	
Describe how you set expectations when delegating and how you monitor progress.	
Negotiation Skills	Evidence of skill level: 1 2 3 4 5
Give me an example of a time when you had to adjust your negotiation tactics to achieve a desired result.	
Describe how you have managed conflict, manipulation, and strong emotions in previous negotiations.	
Other Questions	
The rest of your interview scorecard is comprised of questions you feel are important and appropriate for your company.	
Recommendation	Overall rating: 1 2 3 4 5
❑ More Interviews ❑ Hire/Promote ❑ Do NOT Hire/Promote	
Explanation: Signature: _____	

NOTE: These behavioral-based questions from Descriptions Now software.

When your team interviews the candidate, each one of them takes a share of ownership in the hiring decision. The team then shares responsibility for the candidate's success – VERY IMPORTANT!

Interviewers should be encouraged to ask other questions also. The scorecard provides a standardized tool for all interviewers to compare notes on similar areas of questioning in addition to sharing their conclusions based on their own questioning.

4. **In-person interview**: Once the candidate has passed the phone screen and the assessments are consistent with other top performers in the position (<u>job match</u>), then interview the candidate yourself. If the candidate looks promising to you, then immediately schedule interviews with other people who will be regularly working with the candidate.

5. **Additional interviews**: The candidate should interview with everyone whom he/she will be working with on a regular basis regardless of position – up to 5 or 6 people. We recommend these interviews occur individually – the candidate with one interviewer at a time – however some of our clients like to have the candidate meet with a group. They like to see whether the candidate can survive the pressure, particularly if it is a sales or technical position.

After everyone has interviewed the candidate, have a meeting within 2 days to share your conclusions, including comparing scorecard results.

6. <u>**Confirm accomplishments**</u>: If the candidate claims to have a great talent or to have accomplished something out of the ordinary, then compliment her and ask for people you can call to confirm it. First of all, these contacts can validate the claim. This is important particularly if this claimed skill or accomplishment is going to affect compensation. Secondly these contacts may prove to be people you may want to recruit also, just be careful how you handle it so you do not offend the candidate.

7. **Keep the process moving**: Good candidates do not wait around. If you have confirmed through interviewing this is a good candidate, then quickly validate your conclusion through assessments, background checks and reference checks so you can hire her before someone else does.

Look for people with passion. As Steve Tessler of Checkpoint HR[48] (www.CheckpointHR.com) says, *"If they have passion, they can translate it into your company. If they don't have passion, then they're milk. Vanilla. Plain. You're then forced to instill passion into the person, rather than him/her adding value to your organization."*

Notice Steve's emphasis is on something internal to the person rather than appearance. Instinctively we judge a person based on their looks. This is not only illegal, it is not effective. A potential employee who is going to meet with clients in-person may have an edge if he is attractive, but do NOT be so foolish as to let appearance convince you that he has skills.

Use behavioral-based interview questions, assessments, background checks, reference checks and listening to the candidate describe his accomplishments to understand whether he can accomplish anything for you. *Know the person's values before you hire* – skills can be learned whereas good values often cannot.

NOTE: If you like a candidate after the interviews, then you have to sell the candidate that your job opportunity is better than others she may be considering. <u>Always respond promptly to any communication from a candidate.</u>

I am often asked how long the interview process should take. It varies based on your company. On a recent airplane trip I met Dan Sanders, VP Manufacturing/Operations for Jadoo Power Systems (www.JadooPower.com). They creatively develop and manufacture next generation hydrogen fuel cell technology.

He said his interview process lasted 3-4 days. He also said that as a result of using a comprehensive interview process, their turnover is zero. Plus without any prompting Dan added confidently, *"What we're doing is going to change the world. You just watch."* Dan's company has made certain their employees *Understand How You Make a Difference.*

Other people are trying to cram an entire hiring process into one day because their job market for top talent is so tight. The most important rule is to follow your entire system so you confirm you are not just hiring someone who interviews well. Make certain the person is qualified, will work well with other employees and your team is committed to the candidate's success.

If the candidate seems capable after the initial phone or in-person interview, have him take behavioral and motivators assessments.

#5 - Assessments

Assessments are the next step because your people's time is too valuable to continue interviews prior to assessing the candidate's strengths and weaknesses.

Assessments are becoming more common and candidates accept testing as part of the job qualification process. One firm <u>increased their employee retention rate 400% by using assessments</u> during the hiring process.

There are two key benefits to using assessments:

1. Assessments help you identify the best candidate based on matching them to your existing star performers, and

2. Quality assessments are often defensible in a court of law.

The cost of replacing an employee can be as high as 50-250 percent of their annual salary.

The cost of assessments is pennies compared to the cost of hiring someone who is wrong for the job. This is because hiring the wrong person costs your company lost compensation, overhead, time, and lost opportunity as the process is repeated while no one is doing the work for you full-time.

For instance Golden Corral, a popular family steakhouse chain, was enduring 54 percent annual turnover of general managers. After changing their company's hiring process to something that is similar to *Right Person – Right Job*, their turnover rate dropped to 17 percent in 3 years.

As reported in Workforce Performance Solutions magazine (April 2005), *"Golden Corral CEO Ted Fowler is quick to add* **'In reality, when we lose on of our best GMs, it cost us a million dollars.'** *This is a reflection of the indirect costs that result from disruption* *of business in a successful restaurant, such as lost opportunity, future impact and contribution, higher staff turnover and lower service-quality levels.*"[49]

For others the motivation to use assessments is different. Your lawyers may recommend assessments as part of the hiring process to demonstrate your hiring decisions are without bias.

In the previous chapter we mentioned creating a "job match" of the candidate. The job match compares a completed business personality assessment of the candidate to two documents:

1. The competencies in the job description you wrote to effectively *Pass The Baton on Job Responsibilities.*

2. Assessments of your best employees in a similar position.

Many experts believe a job match successfully identifies potentially excellent employees 75 percent of the time.

Assessments are important because the results help predict how the candidate's behavioral preferences align with the behaviors required for success in a specific job. The result is an increased accuracy of matching the *Right Person* to the *Right Job*.

Recently one assessment company, Profiles International, reported in their newsletter[50] about Aegis Lending. The company has 2,700 employees and 101 branch offices. It lost money one year and then earned $9 million, $23 million and $42 million during the next 3 years. They credited assessments as responsible for at least 25 percent of the profits. That means **assessments contributed $24 million in additional profits** over a 3-year period.[51]

Furthermore, if you use job matching and the assessments are validated to accomplish your goals, then your hiring decisions might be legally defensible in a court of law against claims of discrimination or bias.

What if you try to do a job match against your top two sales people, but you know the only reason one sells a lot is because he is a pushy, hard driving jerk?

If he is a jerk then his competencies are not consistent with your company values. Document the unacceptable behavior, work with him to change, and if he cannot improve to acceptable performance, then fire him. Train your people to avoid being accidentally obnoxious. A growing list of training ideas can be found on our web site.

There is significant difference between quality business personality assessments and just any cheap personality assessment. *Avoid assessments that are "touchy-feely" personality reports.* You need data on how the person behaves in a work environment. Also, when you hire based on a good fit aptitude-wise often you can train the skills necessary to perform the job well.

Continue the interview process if the assessment indicates the person is a match for the job. Do a background check towards the end of completing the interview process.

If the person has potential but is not a match for the position, then conclude the process and maintain her information, or consider her for other openings in your company.

PLEASE NOTE: We have clients who want to make the most of job matching and so we take it a step further. We call this "Job Benchmarking." In this process we take a job and define it with a thorough job description, interview people in the job, assess them, and develop a complete profile of the ideal candidate.

Once you get comfortable with assessments, you can look into adding simulations of work people will do on the job. Develop a proven process with assessments first.

Some studies have shown 2 out of 3 people would rather be working somewhere else or at least doing something else. Leverage assessments to improve your understanding of how to best utilize your existing people. This can have a HUGE positive impact on your bottom line!

You may have employees take assessments and compare the results to the best people in those roles. If they do not match the best profile, the assessment may give you an idea of another position where they may perform better. Lateral moves can improve efficiencies and retention rates.

Studies have found 60 percent of a manager's time is often wasted fixing people problems and only 40 percent is available to focus on helping the company reach its goals. Using quality assessment tools to reduce people-related problems gives managers more time to work on achieving key objectives so your company is better served and your income can grow. [52]

IMPORTANT POINT: An assessment does not enable you to change someone's personality so they are more effective. Also, be careful not to allow assessments to create a situation of bias. *There are more than one type of person who can be successful in a job.* For this reason, when you profile people with assessments to set the standard for a job match, identify your top 2-3 people in each position, not just one person.

Lastly, assessments help you and your employees recognize individual strengths and weaknesses so everyone can adapt behaviors to work better together. (Managers need to help employees focus more activities on their strengths.)

Shandel Slaten,[53] (www.truelifecoaching.com) shared a story about a sales person who is always in a hurry. This sales person would call a project manager and ask a question expecting an immediate answer. The project manager would not reply and the sales person would think the project manager hated her, did not like her work, and disagreed with her recommendation.

In reality, the project manager was just thinking about it. Someone got them together to explain the sales person expects an immediate answer because she personally makes quick decisions. In contrast the project manager thinks carefully before making decisions. Once the sales person understood how the project manager processed information, she adapted her behavior to communicate more effectively.

The story's conclusion is humorous. Now the sales person asks the project manager a question and immediately says, *"I'll call you in 10 minutes for your answer."* The sales person then hangs-up the phone or walks away. It works great. They are not only more productive, but good friends.[54]

If it looks like the assessment(s) indicate a job match, then finish interviewing and do a background check.

#6 – Background Checks

I will not hire someone without doing a background check.

The reason is simple: I have lost too much money hiring people with civil or criminal records that I only discovered after they cost me a lot of money. I could have retired on what I lost. Learn from my mistake and never hire without a background check.

PLEASE NOTE: The smaller your company, the higher the risk. One bad hire could kill your company. For instance, our online system costs about $100 per hire to do a reasonably thorough background check. That is pennies compared to the time you and your staff invested in the hiring process, plus there is the potential damage done by a bad hire.

Make certain your job application states your company reserves the right to do a background check (civil/criminal) and credit report on the candidate. Do not underestimate the potential liability for criminal behavior by an employee. For this reason many companies assess half their employees each year.

Background checks are also cheap compared to costly lawsuits. Recently Penn State University discovered one of its professors committed murder 30 years ago. The Christian Science Monitor reported a Berlin, Germany man failed his driver's test in 1961 and never tried to retake it. For the next 40+ years he worked as a driving instructor.[55] Background checks may save your company from an embarrassing or libelous situation.

I spoke with a retailer recently with over 6,000 employees. He had one employee who stole credit card information from their clients. You would recognize the name of this retailer if I told you. It is world famous, yet this one employee cost them considerable damage. They now do a background check on every employee, even part-timers and seasonal people.

Another option is drug and alcohol testing of your job applicants and existing employees. It is unfortunate, but today many people have substance addictions that are not easy to identify.

The healthcare industry has a big problem in this area because drugs are so easy to obtain on the job. Construction trades, high-end financial jobs and almost every industry can be plagued with this crisis. It may be uncomfortable to test people, but as long as you hold yourself to the same standards, then it may save your company from an embarrassing and/or costly situation.

We offer online background checks that are quick and easy, yet comprehensive. Visit our web site for additional information and a sample job application. If the background check(s) of the candidate meets your standards, then check all of the candidate's references.

#7 – References

Call references on a new hire to confirm her skills, the way she interacts with people, and productivity. Also explain 3-4 typical situations the candidate might face at your company and ask how the person thinks the candidate would respond.

At the end of the conversation, ask the person if there is anyone else she knows who might be willing to share his/her experience of working with the candidate.

Sometimes a former employer refuses to say anything because they fear a lawsuit. For this reason some managers try to find candidates from companies where they know people so they can ask their contacts about the candidate.

It is important to call both professional and personal references. Often times personal references accidentally share information that is very helpful and *either type of reference may turn out to be a good candidate for you to recruit, or someone who can recommend other candidates.*

Background checks and references are particularly important on people in money-handling positions and senior executives.

It is crucial to do your best to hire the *Right Person* for the *Right Job* <u>because people's lives are more important than your profits</u>. For instance, when you hire the wrong person and then fire him, here are some of the ways people can get hurt.

114

Candidate	May miss out on a better job. He is relying on you to buy groceries, pay rent, and have funds for other necessities.
Employees	Your employees have to work harder when you hire the wrong person, fire him, then allocate the candidate's responsibilities to others in addition to their regular duties.
Customers	Your customers want stability and reliable people supporting their relationship with your company. Personnel turnover is confusing and disruptive.

** *Do not hire people just because you like them or you are in a hurry.*

Hire based on aptitude and integrity as indicated by the assessment, the background checks, references, interviews, and everything indicates a job match. This is a more reliable way to hire loyal employees who stay with you through the tough times and tempting offers from other companies.

If you do not check references, then you are not confirming past behavior. *If you do not confirm past behavior, then how can you predict future behavior?*

If the candidate is fully qualified at this point and your team agrees she is the one to hire <u>then immediately get her a written offer!</u>

Onboarding

#8 – Extending the offer

Extend a written offer to the candidate based on agreement by all interviewers that the candidate is the best person for the job <u>and</u> their commitment to support the person's efforts to the best of their ability.

Never extend a verbal offer. Tell a candidate you are prepared to make her an offer and give her the option to meet in person or receive the offer letter via fax, email or postal mail.

If the offer is acceptable to the candidate, she must sign it and return it. If the terms are not acceptable, it is up to you to decide whether to negotiate new terms or decline, and move on to the next candidate. If acceptable, then the process to develop and recruit this person as a long-term employee has just begun.

Lastly, I once received a job offer verbally, but then no offer letter for weeks. Why wait? People have families to feed and bills to pay. My experience is that a procrastinator is a poor manager and the candidate can expect more of the same if he accepts the job.

Remember the Golden Rule is to treat others the way you want to be treated. Keep the hiring process moving! The sooner the person joins your team, the faster he contributes to your bottom line.

#9 – First Day

The First Day is the process of successfully integrating new employees into your firm. After selecting the *Right Person* for the *Right Job*, the first day is critical to the employee's success.

It is simple math: The faster you get the new employee into your system and trained to perform his duties, the earlier you see results to your bottom line from this employee. You also retain more good people when the candidate's First Day is well-organized.

To make the First Day productive and meaningful, make certain **prior to the first day** the new employee has received a Welcome Packet and all paperwork for her to start the position has been completed including assessments, background checks, reference checks, W-4, and other personnel forms.

A Welcome Packet must always be mailed, never handed to the person. The Welcome Packet consists of glossy company brochures and merchandise with your company logo. Its purpose is to convince the people who live with your new employee that she accepted a job with a really great company – *yours*!

They see the color company brochures and have some coffee in a mug you provided and say, *"Wow, this looks like a great company you joined!"* They validate the new employee's decision to come work for you.

Prior to the new employee's First Day, she is entered into your human resource and/or accounting software; she has a desk, phone, office supplies, computer system fully loaded with software, user name and password; I.D. badge and/or business cards; a specific training schedule is set with draft goals for the first 90 days; and she can quickly move into a productive role.

This 90-day plan is particularly important. It's like a 90-day *Success Plan*. You draft it for the employee because the person is new, but make certain she thoroughly understands each objective and agrees to it. Possibly you need the buy-in and commitment of support from others – *then get it!* As the weeks pass make certain you follow-through regularly to help her over any obstacles.

You can define your First Day process in software, as a Word or Excel document, so you implement it consistently each time. It is important that as you continue to hire your professional and highly attractive First Day process is maintained for every new employee. Candidates who learn about your company will expect it and existing employees will take pride in it.

The benefit: The new employee feels wanted, appreciated and her decision to join your firm is confirmed because an organized company is often a winning one. Your business communicates it follows through on its commitments and this motivates the new employee to maintain that same standard.

But do not stop here.

#10 – Do Not Stop Selling

Once you have signed the new employee, do not stop selling him on the value of becoming a productive member of your team.

This starts with how promptly you follow-through each step of the hiring process, including the offer letter, Welcome Packet and pre-employment paperwork. Then it is critical for her first day to have your full attention and when she meets with other team members they are prepared to train her, not just say, "Hi!"

You can compare the new employee's decision to accept the job to deciding to buy a house. There can be "buyer's remorse." The new employee can wonder whether it is the right decision, change his mind, and back out before the first day. Or he may arrive his first day hesitant, waiting to see if you prove he made the right decision to take the job.

The first day is crucial. It is the foundation for your long-term relationship with the employee and no other employee or client crisis can distract you from fully engaging the new employee.

If the start date is not immediate, then schedule a lunch with the new hire to meet and casually discuss his upcoming opportunity and answer any additional questions he may have.

Never stop motivating your employees by helping them to *Understand How You Make a Difference* through true stories, written articles, product or service demonstrations and other interactions about how your company delivers value to your clients.

If 20% of your sales people generate 80% of your profits, then should you replace the other 80% of your sales people?

It may be worth considering replacing weak performers more quickly because now you can leverage these *Desired Results* (and more) to hire and retain truly great people:

- *Understand How You Make a Difference*
- *Pass The Baton on Job Responsibilities*
- *Right Person – Right Job*

Maybe you need to structure a development plan modeled after the proven behaviors of your top 20 percent. Then work with the 80 percent of your team that is underperforming to improve their contribution to your company.

Lastly, hire committed team players more than the most expensive people. Professional football has found out this is true. When the New England Patriots and Philadelphia Eagles were days before the 2005 Super Bowl, the Associated Press quoted Eagles owner, Jeffrey Lurie as saying: *"...Both teams are high-character teams. There are a lot of similar value systems for each team. We each place a high value on the quality of people in our organization."*[56]

Conclusion

The investment you make in each employee is huge. Therefore be wise - invest the time to get the *Right Person* in the *Right Job*.

People are <u>not</u> your greatest asset, however, hiring and developing the *Right People* in the *Right Job* is one of your greatest assets. (Knowledge is the other.)

Knowledge is the intellectual property your people acquire about how your company delivers the best products and services. The *Success With People* system helps you develop knowledge in your people <u>and retain them longer</u>.

Matching the *Right Person* to the *Right Job* enables your business to grow by hiring more qualified people – candidates that can perform like your best folks - through an improved hiring process.

Lastly, interact with your candidates respectfully, promptly and with integrity – *just as you would want if your roles were reversed.* Do not rush your hiring process or procrastinate because either negatively affects the candidate's emotional and financial status.

Following the *Right Person – Right Job* system rewards you with a strong foundational relationship with talented employees who:

- ❑ Have a career, not a job

- ❑ Feel appreciated, not taken for granted

- ❑ Are focused on their work, not looking for another job

You have now learned 7 of the 12 *Desired Results* of the *Success With People* system. Here is what we have covered so far:

<u>Establish Your Foundation</u>

1. *Systematic Power* is a commitment to hire, manage, develop and retain talent systematically.

2. *Understand How You Make a Difference* makes working for your company a meaningful experience and fuels employee passion to achieve.

119

3. *LOI: Live It - Observe It - Improve It* involves your employees with your products to increase their passion for your company and ability to serve clients better.

4. *Sanctuary* combines *Rest, Reflect,* and *Risk* to give you a clearer perspective, renewed energy and inspirational creativity to achieve your best.

Balance Your Workload

5. *Success Plans* help you achieve key goals by balancing personal and professional objectives more effectively.

6. *Pass The Baton on Job Responsibilities* efficiently delegates work to your employees.

7. *Right Person – Right Job* is a complete, proven hiring system to hire the best and avoid the rest.

Notice how we are *Balancing Your Workload* through priority management, effectively delegating work and hiring better people to work with you to fully develop your company.

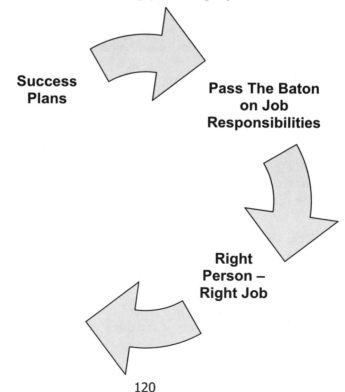

Success Plans

Pass The Baton on Job Responsibilities

Right Person – Right Job

Right Person – Right Job is a complete, proven hiring system to hire the best and avoid the rest. Here is a quick summary.

✓ Save time and money recruiting using your web site and job boards like *Craigslist, Monster* and *CareerBuilder*.

✓ Save time and money recruiting with software to manage the recruiting process – see our web site.

✓ Interview using behavior-based interview questions from software. Visit our web site for our most current recommendation.

✓ Assessments and background checks are essential to identifying the best candidates for specific jobs. Learn more on our web site.

✓ Do criminal and/or civil background checks on key hires – *particularly executives and people handling money.*

✓ Check references.

✓ Make the First Day really special and agree upon a 90-day *Success Plan* so you have mutual expectations.

✓ Be slow to hire - find the best candidate. Proceed through your complete hiring process without procrastinating.

✓ Be quick to fire – not instantaneous – but follow a process to document how he is trained, why he is not right for the job, how his unacceptable performance was communicated to him in writing, and empathetically follow a process to let him go.

Compensation That Pays

And you thought all compensation was pay...

The foundation of *Compensation That Pays* is a delicate balance between managers and employees discussing and coming to agreement about job expectations and how those expectations are achieved. The fulcrum point of this balance, if you picture it like a seesaw or balance beam scale, is the company's commitment to reward employees for their contributions.

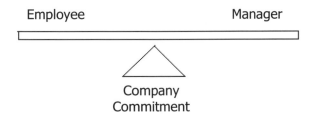

If your company is committed to pay people fairly based on their performance, then you should develop a compensation plan to <u>pay your people with a purpose</u>. One method is to use 4 distinct forms of compensation in a strategic manner to achieve specific objectives.

Compensation That Pays has 3 distinct components: Base Pay, Benefits and Performance Pay.

Base Pay is the person's salary. They get this just for showing up to work.

Benefits are their medical and dental insurance, vacations, etc. They also get this just for being there.

Performance Pay is performance-related awards that must be re-earned each year and does not increase base salary.   Each award is based on the significance of contribution by the employee and/or his team, division or company.

Thousands of companies have used the concept of *Compensation That Pays* for decades. This is often referred to as "total pay," "variable pay," "synchronized pay," and/or "pay for performance." As a matter of fact, it is estimated 80 percent of companies nationwide offer some type of pay-for-performance program, which is performance-related awards that must be re-earned each year and do not increase base salary.[57]

Unlike paying someone just to show up for work, *Compensation That Pays* is flexible, can be customized to fit virtually any business situation, and can be tied directly to specific achievements. For this reason it helps an organization execute more effectively.

It does take some time to structure and administer *Compensation That Pays,* but it is really worth the effort.

How does the *Success With People* system define performance? It varies based on your company, but *performance must always directly or indirectly drive long-term profit.* Profit fuels your ability to compensate employees, exceed customer expectations, and develop the best products.

Hewitt Associates[58] recently found that high growth companies have successful pay-for-performance programs when they provide the appropriate amount of administrative, communication and monetary support. These organizations know this type of pay plan reinforces a performance culture only when it is implemented correctly.

Please note Hewitt Associates found the opposite is true when pay-for-performance fails at a company. In those instances, broad-based employee performance pay is seen as an entitlement to employees and/or a substantial loss to employers. In that situation, the fulcrum point of the balance has moved so the system fails.

Obviously when this occurs you quickly lose your balance, the system fails, and everyone loses. Let me give you 2 examples where *Compensation That Pays* does not work because management is not truly committed to pay for performance.

Example #1 – Manager Bias

Greedy Executives

Typically executives are on some type of pay-for-performance plan. Unfortunately in many cases executives are paid large sums of compensation even when they fail to perform.

The typical CEO now makes $301 for every $1 paid to the typical employee. That has risen astronomically from $42 to $1 in 1982. This means if the typical employee earns $30,000 then the CEO is making $9 million.

When this occurs, a small number of senior executives are paid profits that should be distributed to shareholders as a return on their investment, employees based on their performance, and/or invested for the company to grow.

This type of situation creates an imbalance that is destructive to a company.

Today more than 28 million people, about a quarter of the workforce between the ages of 18 and 64, earn about $9.00 per hour, which means they make less than $19,000 per year. Most do not receive any paid medical or dental insurance, day care for their children, holidays or vacation benefits.[59]

You can improve this statistic by becoming a leader who proves through your actions that you are a great steward of people and physical resources. Find a balance between providing opportunities for all your employees to earn more in return for delivering greater results.

When my grandfather, Chester MacPhee, was a relatively young man it bothered him that rich people could own profitable commercial real estate like shopping centers, but the average person could not. He decided to start a real estate investment trust. He reached out to associations of working people, like fireman, police and tradesmen. He raised millions of dollars and paid cash for properties.

He helped his shareholders make a lot of money. At one point, his real estate investment trust had increased the dividend 26 quarters in a row. He did it by investing carefully, keeping his overhead low and avoiding debt. He made some money by investing himself and receiving a reasonable salary. He worked hard to make certain his shareholders earned a great return on their investment.

You can identify companies that require their managers to work for their employees. One way Costco demonstrates this is on their web site. Click on Investor Relations and then select Code of Ethics.

Under Code of Ethics, there is a list of executive officers – *in alphabetical order!* Typically the company president, James Sinegal, would be listed first or second. Instead he is listed 29th on the list. Costco is known for paying employees well and gives the impression they understand stewardship.

Do not allow Greedy Executives or Foolish Managers to weigh down your company so the balance is removed from your compensation plan (see below).

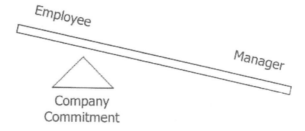

Foolish Managers

Sometimes you have avoided Greedy Executives, but instead have Foolish Managers who are unwilling to allow their employees make more money. Too often they try to use pay-for-performance as a means to not pay for improved productivity.

The Harvard Business Review relates a story about a division within a Fortune 100 company that tried a variable pay plan. The managers launched a program of team goals coupled with team-based pay with three possible levels of reward. The managers projected 90 percent of the teams could reach Level 1, 50 percent could reach Level 2, and only 10-15 percent reach Level 3 (the highest).

For the first six months everyone loved the system and worked harder than ever. The result was the majority of teams reached Level 2 and 3. The company benefited from greater productivity and probably profits. However, the compensation that had to be paid was greater than expected by the managers.

Apparently the managers had no intention of rewarding people for improved performance, but just wanted to pay less for weak performance. Rather than compliment the employees that reached Level 2 and 3, the managers adjusted the goals upward to unreachable heights.

Too many of the objectives were affected by situations out of the control of workers, so the goals could not be achieved. Workers became upset and disillusioned. Shortly thereafter the managers killed the system. Apparently their core objective was not to pay people more; it was only to work people harder.

To succeed with *Compensation That Pays*, you must balance the objective of higher company profits with the opportunity for workers to earn more money.

You must provide each employee an opportunity to share directly in the success of your company.

It always amazes me when managers don't appreciate the greater productivity and profits employees generate <u>if they have to pay for it</u>. Employees are motivated to work harder and smarter to build a better future for themselves, you, and your company when they have an opportunity to share directly in your company's success.

127

Greedy Executives and Foolish Managers are one area where your company can fail your employees and the organization as a whole. In both cases management is not committed to find and maintain a balance within the program, but there is another way *Compensation That Pays* can fail.

Example #2 Employee Bias

The other reason *Compensation That Pays* fails is the other side of the balance scale. Some employees can weigh down your compensation program because they are too lazy. They convince their managers to set goals that are too easy to achieve or not aligned with strategic company objectives.

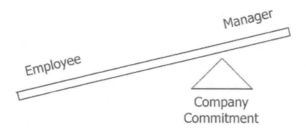

Once again, this situation causes the company to lose balance quickly. This comes about because managers are out of touch with the real productivity available from employees. For people to have meaning in their work and provide profits to your bottom line, you need to find a balance between manager and employee pay objectives.

We are going to use Nucor Steel (www.Nucor.com), an American steel company, as our example for *Compensation That Pays* because they have made it work for decades. There are a variety of ways to pay employees effectively. One way is to adapt what Nucor has done to your firm based on your business model and company culture.

Compensation That Pays is designed for managers to award monetary and recognition awards based on the significance of the contribution of each employee. The employees that contribute more, earn more. It is also important for <u>your managers to be committed to managing the program</u>.

Therefore our starting point is to review Nucor's Management Philosophy.[60] Nucor productively operates steel manufacturing and steel products facilities economically. Their organizational structure has only 4 management layers:

Chairman / Vice Chairman / President

Vice President / General Manager

Department Manager

Supervisory / Professional

Hourly Employee

It may look like 5 layers, but there are only 4 management layers. Hourly Employees do not manage anyone. This streamlined chain of command provides the general managers at each Nucor facility with a lot of autonomy in operating their facility as an independent business.

Day-to-day decisions are made at the operating facilities. Remember how we talked about your employees taking ownership of their job responsibilities? Under this model problems are solved quickly because there is no waiting for an answer from headquarters. Communication is informal and efficient. Employee relations at Nucor are based on 4 simple principles:

1. Management is obligated to manage Nucor in such a way that employees will have the opportunity to earn according to their productivity.

2. Employees should feel confident that if they do their jobs properly, they will have a job tomorrow.

3. Employees have the right to be treated fairly and must believe that they will be.

4. Employees must have an avenue of appeal when they believe they are being treated unfairly.

Do you see how the foundation of the program is focused on **management serving employees** rather than the reverse?

Nucor produces at the highest rates in the industry and their people earn the most of any steelworkers in America. It is important to note Nucor has not laid-off a single worker due to lack of work since they began this program in the 1980's. They take a lot of other steps to build teamwork and make certain their employees are treated as co-owners, not just employees. Nucor employees like the fact the company is non-union because they make more money and do better work setting their own rules.

Nucor provides employees with a unique performance-related compensation system that rewards goal-oriented employees. All employees are covered under one of four basic compensation plans, each featuring incentives related to meeting specific goals and targets. This is where their plan gets exciting.

Production Incentive Plan

Employees involved directly in manufacturing are paid weekly bonuses based on the production of their work group, which range from 20 to 40 workers each. Most Nucor employees are covered under this system.

Typically, these bonuses are based upon anticipated production time or tonnage produced, depending upon the type of facility. The formulas for determining the bonus are non-discretionary, based upon established production goals. This plan creates pressure for each individual to perform well and, in some facilities, is tied to attendance and tardiness standards.

No bonus is paid if equipment is not operating. This creates a strong emphasis on maintaining equipment in top operational condition at all times. Maintenance personnel are assigned to each shift, and they participate in the bonus along with the other bonus groups. Production supervisors are also a part of the bonus group and receive the same bonus as the employees they supervise. In general, the Production Incentive bonus can average 80-150 percent of the base wage.

Production Incentives effectively motivate people because it balances a salary with actual productivity. There is always tremendous power when management and employees work with a balanced objective.

I also like the way Nucor managers and employees have identified various components within the control of the employees that affect productivity and have built those in as components to earn the incentive. Maintaining equipment is one of them.

Department Manager Incentive Plan

Nucor Department Managers earn incentive bonuses paid annually based primarily upon the return on assets of their facility. Nucor pays no discretionary bonuses. All facilities have a common and clear goal since Department Manager bonuses are based upon written plans that are easy to understand. These bonuses can be as much as 82 percent of base salary.

Unlike our Foolish Managers example, Nucor Department Managers do not receive bonuses based on criteria other than production thus <u>everyone is held accountable to the same standard</u>.

Non-Production and Non-Departmental Manager Incentive Plan

This bonus is paid to all employees not on the Production Incentive Plan or the Department Manager Incentive Plan. Participants include accountants, engineers, secretaries, clerks, receptionists or any one of a broad number of different employee classifications.

The bonus is based primarily upon each facility's return on assets. Like all Nucor incentive compensation bonus plans, this bonus is <u>not</u> discretionary. The bonus is based on a clear, understandable written plan that is accessible to employees.

Every month each operation receives a report showing their return on assets on a year-to-date basis. This chart is posted in the employee cafeteria or break area together with the chart showing the bonus payout. The chart keeps employees apprised of their expected bonus levels throughout the year. This bonus can total over 25 percent of salary.

The key is how much more productivity and actual bottom line results can your employees generate to justify earning more money? If your company is making more, then you and the members of your team certainly should earn more. How much more involves details unique to your firm.

Other Employee Bonus Plans

In addition to these established bonus plans, Nucor periodically issues an extraordinary bonus to all employees, <u>except officers</u>, during times when Nucor is enjoying very strong performance. This bonus has been as high as $800 for each employee.

Do you see how Nucor's incentive compensation programs offer each and every employee an opportunity to share directly in Nucor's success? It provides strong encouragement for employees to work hard to build a better future for Nucor and themselves.

Senior Officers Incentive Plan

Nucor senior officers do not have employment contracts. They receive no profit sharing, pension, discretionary bonuses nor retirement plans. Their base salaries are set at less than what executives receive in comparable companies.

The compensation of senior officers is based upon Nucor's return on stockholder equity, above certain minimum earnings. In addition a portion of pre-tax earnings is placed into a pool that is divided among officers in bonuses that are about 60% stock and 40% cash.

If Nucor does well, the officer's compensation is well above average, as much as several times base salary. If Nucor does poorly, the officer's compensation is only base salary and, therefore significantly below the average pay for this type of responsibility.

In the good years, Nucor executives do make millions, but the <u>shareholders and employees have been paid first</u> before the executives.

Compare this to a giant media corporation recently paying their president and chief operating officer $30 million of shareholders' money to resign after less than 2 years on the job. Or another major corporation firing their CEO and paying the executive $21 million to leave. **Why are people rewarding executives so highly for failure?** Possibly the typical Board of Directors has lost sight of the importance of protecting the company's cash resources. The fired executive makes a bundle while the company, employees and shareholders all suffer.

There is another reason Nucor's compensation plan for their top executives is super. Their senior executives do not enjoy company cars, corporate jets, executive dining rooms, executive parking places and other perks many of those overpaid executives have. *Employees actually enjoy some benefits executives do not have.*

Unique Employee Benefits

The Nucor Scholarship Program provides four-year scholarships for children of Nucor employees pursuing higher education or vocational training past high school. The program pays up to $2,500 annually for each qualified student. All children of employees can qualify.

Jim Collins in *Good to Great* tells a story about one Nucor employee with 8 children. When his manager confirmed all 8 children would receive scholarships, the employee cried. You might cry for joy too if your company just promised you $80,000 tax-free for your children's education!

The employees also receive profit sharing, an employee stock purchase plan, extraordinary bonus and service awards that are not available to the officers. <u>Everyone</u> has the same holidays.

Your company may have a unique benefit offering a dual value to your company and employees. For instance Google <u>insists</u> all engineers have one day a week to work on their own pet projects. They even have an ideas mailing list for people to post proposals. *It is better to fund your in-house entrepreneurs than have them make someone else wealthy.*[61]

Do not exactly copy what Nucor has done. Consider this:

❏ Executives must serve their employees and shareholders before themselves. When executives are paid extra compensation, it needs to be from the surplus after employees and shareholders have made a reasonable return. <u>This is the ethical thing to do.</u> *Stop talking about values and ethics –* demonstrate them through your actions.

How you manage <u>company</u> money tells others what type of person you really are, and how you serve them.

❑ You must pay for performance. *Your employees should share in the benefits in direct proportion to how much they helped create the increased profits.*

Structure compensation based on performance so your smartest, most hard working, resourceful people can make unlimited money. Reward the developer of the next generation product or the operations manager who delivers a breakthrough that saves the company millions. Pay the reward over time as the savings occur. This way the employee is motivated to stay with your company rather than the instant gratification of a one-time bonus.

Notice how Nucor's program is in direct contrast to the Foolish/Greedy Manager and Lazy Employee approach? **Employees struggling to pay bills are <u>not</u> motivated to perform their best when executives are overpaid.**

A Balanced Approach

Make certain your compensation plan does the following:

1. **Balance**: Establish *Compensation That Pays* plans for all employees, including executives, that pay beyond minimum levels only when the individual performance warrants it.

2. **Meaning**: Make certain your employees *Understand How They Make a Difference* (*Desired Result #2*). The Harvard Business Review has stated, *"People do work for money – but they work even more for meaning in their lives. In fact, they work to have fun. Companies that ignore this fact are essentially bribing their employees and will pay the price in a lack of loyalty and commitment."*[62]

3. **Recognition**: Your employees want to be recognized and appreciated. *Study after study has proven people are not motivated by money alone.* Beyond recognition in front of peers gifts should support the employee's personal interests.

One man shared the story of how he was awarded an Employee of the Year award for his department. He got a plaque and no cash. Every time he looked at the plaque, he was reminded how he did not get any cash. It really bothered him. When asked what would have been a better solution, he explained it would have meant a lot to him to receive a high quality gift related to his personal hobby. Then the plaque would have reminded him of the thoughtfulness of his firm to recognize his contribution.

4. **Freedom**: Allow your employees some freedom to set and pursue goals that enable the company to achieve its objectives. Give them ownership, support their effort and motivation will soar.

ESOP

An Employee Stock Ownership Plan (ESOP) is an employee benefit plan which makes the employees owners of stock in your company. An ESOP is an employee benefit. A 401K program invests in many companies whereas an ESOP is required by law to invest primarily in the securities of the sponsoring employer.

Employees of an ESOP company may partially own, control a majority share or totally own the company. Many large corporations have ESOP programs, including Proctor & Gamble, SAIC, Anheuser-Busch, and Brookshire Brothers.

The ESOP Association reports Dr. Douglas Kruse, an expert on ESOPs, assembled 30 of the most recent studies on ESOPs and concluded ESOP companies on average beat similar non-ESOP companies by 4 to 5% on productivity measures.[63]

The National Center for Employee Ownership says major academic studies show companies with ESOPs grow in sales, employment, and productivity by 2% to 3% per year faster than the companies would have without an ESOP.

Nevertheless, for ESOPs to succeed companies need to combine broad ownership with an "ownership culture" that gives employees more influence in day-to-day decisions and shares corporate performance data with employees in a detailed, regular manner.[64]

The ESOP merely confirms management is committed to serving employees by giving them ownership in the organization. However this "ownership culture" is really driven by how you manage people on a day-to-day basis.

Barry MacLean, a nationally recognized compensation expert observes:

"To be successful your compensation program must be designed to mirror and reinforce your management style and culture; not be a replacement for it. Your company doesn't become successful like Nucor because of its compensation program, but rather because of the management style and culture which is reflected by the compensation program.

"Too many companies make the mistake of thinking if they can just get their incentive program tuned perfectly they won't have to manage. This is particularly prevalent in sales compensation. It is a recipe for sure disaster, especially in the rapid change world in which we work."

Compensation That Pays is just one *Desired Result* of an overall system for effectively managing people. It requires focused attention to develop, test, implement, refine and re-introduce a successful pay program, but it is valuable only when it supports the other *Desired Results* of your *Success With People* system.

Consider your *Compensation That Pays* plan very carefully. Discuss your draft plan with your employees before implementing it for a trial period. Make certain you hold yourself and other managers accountable to similar performance standards.

Conclusion

How you pay your employees, managers and senior executives communicates more about your company values than anything else you do. Too often today the compensation paid to the top 5-10 executives is excessively obscene. **You can leave a better legacy**.

Bruce Murphy in the Milwaukee Journal Sentinel recently reported, *"J.P. Morgan once said no chief executive should earn more than 20 times an average worker's pay."* And he added:

"... If average worker pay, which is now $26,899, had risen like CEO pay, it would exceed $184,000. If the minimum wage had risen at the same rate, it would now be almost $45 an hour." [65]

Barry MacLean likes to say: **"Compensation is the ultimate communication tool."** *What do you want to communicate to your employees?*

NOTE: Do not rely on compensation alone to drive improved performance. If you do, you may improve performance but your employee turnover rate will be high because working for you is just a job. Make certain you are working the *Desired Results* of the first suite, *Establish Your Foundation*.

WARNING: Often people need to move into this type of program in increments than a major radical move all at once. You may want to talk with one of our consultants or an advisor you trust who has expertise in this area.

Congratulations! *Compensation That Pays* completes the *Balance Your Workload* suite. Here is what you have learned so far.

Establish Your Foundation

1. *Systematic Power* is a commitment to hire, manage, develop and retain talent systematically.

2. *Understand How You Make a Difference* makes working for your company a meaningful experience and fuels employee passion to achieve.

3. *LOI: Live It - Observe It - Improve It* involves your employees with your products to increase their passion for your company and ability to serve clients better.

4. *Sanctuary* combines *Rest, Reflect,* and *Risk* to give you a clearer perspective, renewed energy and inspirational creativity to achieve your best.

Balance Your Workload

5. *Success Plans* help you achieve key goals by balancing personal and professional objectives more effectively.

6. *Pass The Baton on Job Responsibilities* efficiently delegates work to your employees.

7. *Right Person – Right Job* is a complete, proven hiring system to hire the best and avoid the rest.

8. *Compensation That Pays* motivates your people by paying them as co-owners while demonstrating company values through your actions.

Therefore here is one way to *Balance Your Workload.* It involves focusing on key objectives, effectively delegating work, hiring better people and compensating people in such a way that they take control of their destiny with your company passionately.

Keep this "flywheel," as Jim Collins likes to call it, cycling faster and faster to empower your people to achieve their dreams while also enabling your company to post record results.

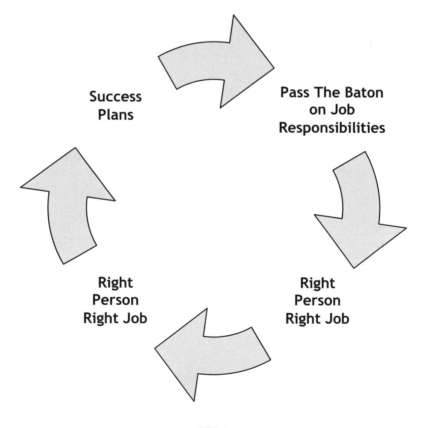

Success Plans

Pass The Baton on Job Responsibilities

Right Person Right Job

Right Person Right Job

Compensation That Pays motivates your people by paying them as co-owners while demonstrating company values through your actions. Here is a quick summary.

✓ Most important: Establish a management philosophy that commits managers to serve employees.

✓ Commit yourself and your management team to allow employees to earn more in exchange for delivering higher quality work and/or greater results.

✓ Divide your compensation plan into base pay, benefits, variable pay, and recognition pay.

✓ Remove any executive perks, such as special benefits, cars, first-class airfare, etc.

✓ Outline your initial thoughts on how a pay-for-performance plan might work in your company. Do not allow your employees to design the plan, but allow them to provide input.

✓ Consider the Balanced Approach on page 134.

✓ When announcing the plan make certain you explain how they will be able to achieve the objectives and provide the support they need to succeed.

✓ How you pay your employees, managers and senior executives communicates your company values more than anything else you do.

Manage Your Team's Performance

Coach - Do Not Play

Listen More

Halftime Reviews

Goals That Work

Listen More

The final suite of the *Success With People* system is *Manage Your Team's Performance*. Using software to implement these last 4 *Desired Results* saves time, but you can do them manually.

The reason I recommend software to accomplish the *Manage Your Team's Performance* suite is because I have personally used software to *save 10 hours a year per employee managed* using the *Success With People* system. You can check our website for current recommendations.

People react positively to a consistent management style, and the way you lead others is more consistent when you prioritize your management activities with well-designed software.

By this time you should be making great progress in your abilities and results as a manager. This suite of *Desired Results* completes your education of a proven <u>system</u> for effectively managing people.

This *Desired Result* is named, *Listen More*. The focus is talking with your employees, <u>listening</u> and considering their responses, and when appropriate, documenting employee behavior. Noting behavior communicates appreciation for a job well done, or it helps the employee understand you are serious about your request for change. It also provides written backup in an employee lawsuit.

Terminating employees always will be the most hated job of managers. Yet sometimes termination helps people comprehend areas of their life where they need to change and/or lead them to a more personally fulfilling job. **Never fire someone unless you first have detailed documentation supporting the dismissal.**

As part of any process and communication about events with employees, remember there are legal risks involved in managing people. Many of these liabilities can be avoided by documenting behavior carefully, yet quickly in software.

In a recent year there were over 80,000 claims of discrimination filed with the Equal Employment Opportunity Commission, just one of over 50 agencies responsible for investigating these claims.[66] The EEOC collected over $300 million in fines from companies like yours. Document employee behavior carefully. Do not take chances in this area.

Another term for documenting behavior is Log Events. Identifying Log Events is part of how to *Listen More*. Spend time with employees to *Listen More* about the work they do, their opinion of your business, and their evaluation of working with other employees.

Marshall Goldsmith, the well-known executive coach, recently commented in his column for Workforce Performance Solutions magazine, *"Howard Morgan and I recently published a study involving more than 11,000 leaders and 86,000 of their co-workers from eight major corporations. Our findings were clear:*

"Leaders who ask, listen, learn and consistently follow up are seen as becoming more effective.
Leaders who don't ask don't get much better."

These Log Events also provide a convenient method of documenting performance. Events such as being tardy, not completing a project on time, offending a customer, or dressing inappropriately all might be negative Log Events. Positive Log Events might be completing training, receiving a compliment from a customer, helping a co-worker, or doing something extra around the office.

Part of *Listen More* is recognizing an event is worth recording. The feedback part is to make certain your employee is congratulated or corrected in a positive manner.

No response and delayed responses are the worst form of communication. This discourages good behavior and encourages poor behavior. Do you think any sport would survive without scoring points or audience cheers to encourage winning behavior?

Lack of encouragement is one of the key reasons employees leave your company. You cannot afford to wait until performance review time to interact with employees about their work activities.

Too often performance reviews are written only considering the events of the last month or two. Entering Log Events on a regular basis enables you to review significant events over the past year at review time and provide a more balanced perspective of what the employee has accomplished.

The format for a Log Event is quick and simple:

1. Title the Log Event so when viewing it in a list you can see the date and brief description of what occurred.

2. Event Description: Enter a brief explanation of what happened and the date it occurred.

3. Employee Discussion: Discuss the Log Event with your employee. Document a summary of the conversation and the date it occurred.

Be careful not to write too much detail. Find a balance. One sentence or two is sufficient unless the event is a significant step towards promotion or termination.

Teach your people to give you proper feedback by setting a good example. Be specific in your Log Events rather than write an opinion.[67]

Avoid saying things like, *"Ralph was late today."* That could be considered an opinion. Instead say something like, *"Ralph arrived at 8:50 a.m. this morning when his start time is 8:30 a.m. This is the second time he has been late this week. He was also about 15 minutes late on Monday."*

Discuss the specifics with the employee. Then add notes of the discussion, record the changes he agreed to make, when these changes are to take place and how this poor behavior is to be avoided in the future. Keep it brief.

If you believe it is necessary to warn the employee of repercussions should the poor behavior continue, then write up the Log Event and print it out from the software to have the employee sign it. Place an original copy signed by the employee in their employment file as a written warning.

Sincerely compliment your people often. Announce achievements to others via email, in meetings, posters on the walls, anything that helps build the team. Jesus taught *"For whoever exalts himself will be humbled, and whoever humbles himself will be exalted."*[68] Rather than promote yourself, demonstrate you are serving your people by enthusiastically proclaiming the achievements of others.

Do you realize 65% of Americans received no praise or recognition at work during a recent year (Gallup Poll) and the #1 reason people quit their job is they do not feel appreciated (U.S. Dept. of Labor).[69]

Use Log Events to quickly and easily document good behavior too!

When to Document Behavior

You should recognize or praise behavior weekly if possible, but not all of these events should be documented. Every month or two is typical for Log Events.

There are two types of Log Events:

- ❑ Community: Building community and validating your employees by listening to their perspective on you, your people and your business.

- ❑ Event: Documenting positive or negative events that might support a change in compensation, position or employment.

146

For Community Log Events, take time on a weekly basis to invite an employee out for a walk or a refreshing snack just to hear what might be on their mind. Too often employees only talk among themselves. Their thoughts, concerns, and ideas never make it to the manager. One-on-one meetings are best. Let the employee do most of the talking. You *Listen More*. Talk only to ask or answer questions. You may find your employees suggesting ideas, books, articles and other items to improve your perspective and managerial skills.

For instance, once a quarter the 23 corporate officers of JetBlue go to a city and listen to the airport staff. Does your company have executives asking people working on the front lines with customers, *"What are your challenges each day?"[70]* Are your managers (and you) listening to the responses <u>and giving them full consideration</u>?

> PLEASE NOTE: If you encourage your employees to be candid, at times their feelings are shared in a manner that is offensive. Part of this may be poor communication skills and part may be you do not like what they are saying.
>
> When this happens, calmly listen and take written or mental notes of what is being said. Do not rebuke them or get angry. Ask questions – remember, *Listen More*. Then explain you want to think about what they said and respond at a later date. THANK THEM for sharing their opinion(s). Be committed to not penalize anyone for being candid. Then give yourself time to think about it.
>
> Working through some issues can be challenging. The bottom line is your company is stronger if you gain insight from employees throughout your organization rather than just at the top. Often those entry level employees are the ones interacting most with your customers. They have insights you need to hear and consider to succeed.

Recording events is very important. If you want to fire someone, you need to have documentation the person has not been performing well. Without this documentation, your company is liable for a lawsuit. You also need documentation to support a promotion because someone else in the organization may feel discriminated against when a peer is promoted instead of him.

Always notify the employee of positive Log Events. Most of the time you should notify the employee of negative Log Events, and in many cases it is beneficial to have the employee confirm he has been notified of poor performance. The employee may disagree, but make certain your facts are correct and allow him to document why he disagrees also.

Avoid getting carried away with documenting everything so it becomes like second-guessing your employee's every move. This destroys their confidence. It would be like a high school basketball coach with every player's parent sitting behind her assessing every comment the coach makes to the team. Too much documentation is distracting. You want to primarily document events leads to promotion or termination.

Many years ago a man was asked to become the chairman of the board for a non-profit company in my local community. This company was having serious trouble. The board meetings were long affairs, often lasting until one or two o'clock in the morning as the top executive fought it out with the board members and everyone had to have their say. It was unproductive and contrary to the values of the organization.

To start his initial meeting as chairman, my friend said: *"I have two rules on how these meetings will proceed. First, each meeting will end at 11:00 p.m., even if someone is mid-sentence. Therefore please keep your comments brief and try not to repeat what others have already said. Second, if you have something negative to say, you must first say three sincere, positive things."*

He then enforced those rules. The situation turned around rapidly. Notice my friend had carefully considered the situation and then focused on the positive. Human nature leads many people to build themselves up by putting others down. *Being negative does not get results long-term.*

Many companies document behavior but only in extreme negative situations. Use a balanced approach that documents events leading up to a major positive or negative situation. Watch your Log Events as they grow in your system. If you have a lot more negative Log Events than positive, either you have a bad employee that needs to be let go, or you are struggling to balance your perspective with catching people doing things right.

Business people like to receive communication in different ways. Here are 4 of the most common.

1. Verbal. Some employees are motivated by positive verbal affirmation verbally from their boss, peers and customers.

2. Gifts. Others like to be recognized in written form or gifts.

3. Quality Time. Many prefer you demonstrate they are valuable by spending time with them focused solely on their needs.

4. Acts of Service. Others enjoy acts of service where your actions clearly demonstrate you believe they are important.

Ideally you communicate to your people in all of these ways, but people respond to different methods as their primary means of communication. Gary Chapman has written a number of books on how to communicate you care about others. He calls the series, *The 5 Love Languages.*[71] Possibly some of his research also applies to how a manager should relate to her employees.

Let me close with a story. On a business trip a few years ago I was sitting alone having dinner at a plush hotel restaurant. A family came in and the father asked for a table where their conversation would not bother anyone. As the group of kids passed, I understood why. One of their three children was riding in a special wheelchair that provided extensive body support. He was handicapped in some way.

This young man in the wheelchair talked almost constantly. I could not understand anything he said in part because I was seated a few tables away. The young man's gentle words kept babbling on. I was reading. The noise did not bother me.

About 15 minutes later his words suddenly caught my attention as I heard the young handicapped man saying clearly and strongly, *"I love Mom. I love Mom. I love Mom..."* over and over again.

Tears welled up in my eyes as I gave thanks for this wonderful family who were working so hard to love this child and make him comfortable.

This story is a reminder your employees sometimes lack skills you desire, yet many of them are doing their best. Work to develop your people with training, mentoring, and sincere, specific positive affirmation to help them become better contributors to your company and provide improved service to your customers.

Sometimes your efforts to develop an employee do not succeed. I suggest there is still a benefit. When you look back on this situation in the future you can have peace of mind and meaning in knowing you did your best to fulfill your mutual goal of a productive business relationship.

Birthdays

Birthdays are a natural excuse to tell an employee you appreciate her. Have your assistant remind you, or track all employee birthdays in your Outlook calendar. You may want to track them a day in advance to make certain you send them a note on time.

Before you write them a note, <u>look at their assessment</u> so you are reminded of how best to communicate to the employee.

You may also want to talk with the person's direct supervisor to confirm what is most appreciated about the employee's attitude or behavior <u>separate of performance</u>. It is inappropriate and even insulting to compliment work performance in a birthday greeting. It is okay to include a comment like *"It's great to have you on the team."* This just should not be the primary message.

The best communication is a high quality birthday card, flowers, balloons or a small amount of cash. Just be consistent with every employee. *The quality of the card and the sincerity of your handwritten note are most important.* If you cannot leave a handwritten note on the person's desk or mail it to him, then send a personal email focused on the individual. In other words, do not send a greeting to an employee that includes your favorite quote if it might offend the person personally.

Conclusion

No one purposefully hires someone who gives them grief, but unfortunately all of us come to work with emotional baggage from our past experiences. Do not judge others too quickly. Most people can be star performers if they are in the right job and managed effectively.

WARNING: If you get angry, you lose. Documenting behavior must not be about your ego. It is about recording the facts on resources you have been given to steward – company assets including people.

Chose the *Right Person* for the *Right Job* to the best of your ability, then patiently use the *Success With People* system to develop each employee to perform well for your company. Try to *Listen More* and consider a perspective that may not be easily apparent before letting him go.

Think of what you might have been able to accomplish thus far in your life if someone more experienced had spent the time to *Listen More* to you. How many mistakes might you have avoided? How much pain could you have prevented even though your intentions were good?

Give the gift of *Listen More* to your employees. Teach them how to *Listen More* to others. Your customers will love it too!

As part of listening, document employee behavior at least quarterly so you avoid guessing about their behavior and achievements when writing their performance review.

You have now learned the first *Desired Result* of the *Manage Your Team's Performance* suite.

Establish Your Foundation

1. *Systematic Power* is a commitment to hire, manage, develop and retain talent systematically.

2. *Understand How You Make a Difference* makes working for your company a meaningful experience and fuels employee passion to achieve.

151

3. *LOI: Live It - Observe It - Improve It* confirms how to make your products and services the best they can be, and is a key way to develop passion among your employees.

4. *Sanctuary* combines *Rest, Reflect,* and *Risk* to give you a clearer perspective, renewed energy and inspirational creativity to achieve your best.

Balance Your Workload

5. *Success Plans* help you achieve key goals by balancing personal and professional objectives more effectively.

6. *Pass The Baton on Job Responsibilities* efficiently delegates work to your employees.

7. *Right Person – Right Job* is a complete, proven hiring system to hire the best and avoid the rest.

8. *Compensation That Pays* motivates your people by paying them as co-owners while demonstrating company values through your actions.

Manage Your Team's Performance

9. *Listen More* involves regular interaction with employees to learn from them, show appreciation and document behavior to support promotions or dismissals.

The first *Desired Result* of this "flywheel" is to focus you on listening as well as telling employees what to do. Remember your people represent you to clients and fellow employees.

Their opinions deserve your full consideration and your sincere listening sets an important example for how they need to listen to your clients.

Listen More

152

Listen More involves regular interaction with employees to learn from them, show appreciation and document behavior to support promotions or dismissals. Here is a quick summary.

✓ Give your people opportunities to share their thoughts, ideas and dreams. Listen carefully and consider what is said prior to responding.

✓ Document employee performance that may support promotion or termination

✓ Document events such as customer complaints/ compliments, or non-goal specific achievements.

✓ Keep each Log Event brief, but make certain it includes the facts.

✓ Check yourself to make certain you are balanced in your recording of Log Events, assuming there is both positive and negative behavior to record.

✓ Use software to document behavior (Log Events) quickly and easily. Visit our web site for our most current recommendation.

Goals That Work

Desired Result #10

The *Success With People* system is more than improving employee performance. <u>It is about positively impacting their lives.</u> The way you manage others contributes significantly to their quality of life and the way they *relate to others in their personal life.*

This is one of my favorite *Desired Results - Goals That Work.* Software can be used to save time or you can follow my recommended format manually.

I recently heard Steven Covey speak.[72] He said only 49 percent of U.S. workers understand how their activities contribute to their company reaching its goals (www.FranklinCovey.com).

Furthermore Covey's company, Franklin-Covey, reports only 19 percent of U.S. workers have clearly defined work goals.[73] No wonder we struggle to get things done! There are 3 ways for people to write *Goals That Work.*

Our starting point is reviewing some general guidelines to writing goals. Because consistency is important, your goals should be tied to achieving your company's mission and strategic objectives.

Your Employees

Writing goals for your employees and then telling them what to do without their input removes motivation to do their best. They lack ownership in the goal and as a result they miss some of the passion necessary to achieve great things.

Try this instead:

1. Explain your company goals for the year or upcoming review period to your experienced employees.

2. Ask them to identify how they can help the company achieve these objectives by writing the first draft of their goals.

3. Then meet with them to make certain their goals are consistent with your objectives, aligned with your company goals, and are tasks they can actually achieve. This transforms you from being a dictator to becoming a mentor helping them accept realistic, specific goals.

Assuming your employees have a solid understanding of their responsibilities for the upcoming review period, it is in your best interests to let them lead the process. Remember: *Achieving goals is equally the responsibility of the employee and the manager.*

The Manager

The traditional method of goal writing is the manager writes the goals and then tells the employee what she wants him to achieve. Although the manager's involvement is crucial to the process, try encouraging your experienced employees write the first draft as outlined above or try the process below.

Having the employee involved in the process significantly increases the potential for success, and you may find your employees coming up with important goals or methods to achieve key objectives that you overlooked.

Shared Process

Invite a small employee group to meet. Discuss the objectives for the company and/or your group during the upcoming year and how to achieve them. Have your employee(s) participate in the discussion to identify and assign individual goals.

Goals need to be written so it is clear how success is measured. Do not be lazy and write goals in a brief manner under the excuse of being too busy and/or everyone understands the tasks to be completed.

Start writing your goal with a Goal Title. This is brief so the goal's purpose is known at a glance. Write a date for the goal to be achieved.

If you want to prioritize certain goals over others, then use Goal Weighting. For instance, assume you give a salesperson three goals. The first goal is to close 10 sales this month; the second is to show-up on time; and the third is to dress professionally.

Obviously closing 10 sales is the most important goal to achieve. Therefore you might weight that goal as 80 percent and the other two goals as 10 percent each. Goal Weighting during a review period must total 100 percent and should affect compensation.

Goal Weighting communicates to the employee the goal to close 10 sales is significantly more important than the others.

Close 10 sales	80%
Show-up on time	10%
Dress professionally	10%
Total	100%

There are two components to writing *Goals That Work*.

❑ **Goal Measurement** is a statement enabling both manager and employee to have a clear, mutual understanding of what result constitutes achievement of the goal. <u>If you learn nothing else about writing goals from this book, enjoy this simple formula and write every goal this way</u>.

I call this process writing "TARGET™" goals. Start with the preposition "To" and follow it with an "Action verb." Next add a "Realistic Goal" area or focus. Then add an "Effective measure of success" and close it with the "Time for the goal to be completed."

T	To (the preposition)
A	Action verb
RG	Realistic Goal to be achieved
E	Effectively measure the goal has been achieved
T	Time or date for the goal to be completed

My friend, T.C. Michalak says, *"A goal without a timeline is not a goal – it's a wish."* Have a due date and stick to it.

Here is an example: *To increase the number of widgets produced without error by 10 percent before the end of the quarter.*

To begin:	To
Action verb:	increase*
Realistic Goal:	the number of widgets produced
Effective measurement:	without error by 10 percent
Time bound:	before the end of the quarter.

* Notice the action verb is positive? Write goals so the positive contribution to the company and/or your customers is clear when the goal is achieved.

This is a Russell original inspired by an explanation by Rich Franklin of KnowledgePoint and studying several other methods. When you write a goal this way it is easy for both the manager and the employee to be clear about what meets job requirements (achieves the goal).

TARGET goals are consistent with the SMART method of goal writing – <u>TARGET goals are just easier to write</u> because they define how to write the goal in a sentence.

Teach your people how to write goals using the TARGET method and then help fine-tune the goals so each is realistic and written as a true TARGET objective.

The system for your people to achieve goals is to write their long-term goals as part of the *Top Ten* of their *Success Plan.* Then their *Do It Now* and *Other Achievements* lists contain activities focused on completing steps that eventually enable them to achieve their *Top Ten* goals.

Remember, <u>a successful business operates upon a series of systems that are continuously reviewed and refined to improve efficiencies.</u> Managers and employees must be trained and held accountable to use proven systems, including a solid system for writing *Goals That Work*.

Success With People is powerful because it is a <u>system</u> rather than just an assortment of disconnected actions.

Should business conditions change, then your goals may need to be updated or replaced. However, TARGET goals are typically written for a limited timeframe ranging from one month to one year. Most of the time changes are not required.

Write your goals to meet three requirements:

- The responsibilities are within the employee's authority.

- The desired outcomes can be observed or measured during the review period.

- The tasks are achievable based on the skills, knowledge, resources and/or tools of the employee.

❑ **Goal Description** is the second component of writing *Goals That Work*. The Goal Description breaks the Goal Measurement down into tasks, action items and/or milestones that ultimately result in achieving the goal.

You may also want to specify what results qualify as exceeding job requirements or outstanding performance whereas the Goal Measurement sets forth the level of performance that meets job requirements.

For instance, Dell Computer is always on a mission to outdo itself. As reported in Fast Company Magazine,[74] Dell has brought a maniacal focus to shaving minutes off the time it takes to assemble and ship a computer. If Dell were writing *Goals That Work*, Dell might have a goal

159

where the Goal Measurement is, *"Increase the number of boxes shipped to 400 a day by the end of the quarter."*

In the Goal Description area the Dell manager might encourage employees to study tapes of "the build," look for ways to lower the times a worker touches the computer, identify ways to reduce the number of screws and increase the components that can be snapped in place. These specifics help your employees to focus on key actions to achieving the goal.

Therefore ask your employees to write their draft TARGET goals. When you meet with them first agree upon a final version of the Goal Measurement. Then together define the action steps or tasks necessary to achieve the goal under Goal Description. <u>Put due dates on each step to make certain you stay on track.</u>

The Goal Measurement – the TARGET Goal statement – basically defines what achieving the goal looks like. In a similar way the Goal Description provides a map of how the employee is going to get from where she is today to success with each goal.

The challenge is not writing the goals. It is exciting for employees to document their objectives. <u>The real challenge is for managers to follow-up regularly</u> on the employee's progress achieving the goal.

Not achieving goals is often a symptom of having the wrong person in the job, unrealistic goals being set, and/or no manager follow-up and support. This is the fault of the manager, the employee, or both. Avoid unrealistic goals from your boss and do not place impossible goals on your team.

To effectively manage people you cannot hide behind excuses of being too busy to follow-up on goals you helped create and assigned to others. As a manager your responsibility is to make certain the goals are achieved, and to document the individual's progress towards achieving the goals.

Managers have told me confidently, *"I manage my people with a long leash."* Translation: They do not know how to manage and rarely follow-up on the objectives they set with their people.

Too often managers set goals for their team and then do nothing until performance review time. You are a "manager," which means you have to manage the process not pass it off like an American football. Effective management is like good soccer: The more passing (interaction) between players (employees and their manager), the better the team.

An I.T. manager would never let one of her development projects go for a year, a quarter or even a month without some sort of check on its progress. Financial managers would not go for extended periods of time without checking the progress of their investments. A good sales manager checks in with her account executives regularly. Managers are much more effective when they regularly check the progress people are making to achieve their goals.[75]

Not only must you check the progress your people are making on achieving their goals, but you need to document their progress. This is done quickly and easily in the software. This is important because those Goal Progress Notes help support bonuses, promotions, and motivate your team to succeed. They can also help in the case of termination. You should also let employees enter their own Goal Progress Notes – give them ownership!

How many goals should each employee have?

It depends on the employee, but let me share a checklist that was inspired by the book, *Everyone's a Coach* by Don Shula and Ken Blanchard[76] and parts of which I have seen validated elsewhere. This checklist helps you make certain you always create *Goals That Work*.

#1 – Focused effort - *limit the number of goals.*

Limit long-term goals per employee to a maximum of 5 in any given performance review period. Obviously there must be short-term objectives and assignments, but 3-5 goals are an achievable number. A manager once showed me 17 goals he had been given by his boss for the upcoming year. Many were major projects. That is not reasonable or realistic. He failed to do a good job on any of them.

#2 – Reach the goal - *systematically coach to help the employee master the assignment.*

Stay engaged coaching and mentoring your employees as needed. Do not take on responsibility for achieving your employee's goals, but do your job to help them stay focused on key steps to achieving their goals and overcome obstacles. This is why we talked about Goal Progress Notes and following up regularly.

#3 – Error reduction - *identify & help people overcome errors.*

This supports #2. Your job as a manager is to help your people avoid and overcome errors. You need to communicate to your people what know and what they can learn from others. This requires discipline from both you and your employees. It also requires defining, implementing, and evolving proven systems or processes to achieve key objectives. Expect errors, yet never stop working to perfect systems to avoid errors altogether.

#4 – Excellence - *always strive for perfection, yet accept continuous improvement.*

We ask imperfect people to produce perfect results. It may happen occasionally, but perfection cannot be expected. Constantly seek continuous improvement so excellence may be achieved. Don Shula started every football season coaching the Miami Dolphins with a goal to win every game. How many times did he achieve that goal?

Don Shula's Miami Dolphins won every game and the Super Bowl in only one season. He remains the only coach in the history of NFL football to have accomplished that goal.

Writing *Goals That Work* instills more passion and effectiveness into your team. Passion in today's competitive marketplace is a strategic edge. Employee passion also enables you to delegate more responsibility to others to give you time for other priorities.

Conclusion

Follow these steps to creating goals that are aligned with your company's key objectives, mentoring your team to achieve them, and documenting their progress. Goals are exciting, but not nearly as thrilling as achieving your key objectives each year.

You have now learned how to write and manage *Goals That Work*. Empower your people to reasonably stretch themselves with their goals and your *Desired Results* can be achieved more often.

Establish Your Foundation

1. *Systematic Power* is a commitment to hire, manage, develop and retain talent systematically.

2. *Understand How You Make a Difference* makes working for your company a meaningful experience and fuels employee passion to achieve.

3. *LOI: Live It - Observe It - Improve It* involves your employees with your products to increase their passion for your company and ability to serve clients better

4. *Sanctuary* combines *Rest, Reflect,* and *Risk* to give you a clearer perspective, renewed energy and inspirational creativity to achieve your best.

Balance Your Workload

5. *Success Plans* help you achieve key goals by balancing personal and professional objectives more effectively.

6. *Pass The Baton on Job Responsibilities* efficiently delegates work to your employees.

7. *Right Person – Right Job* is a complete, proven hiring system to hire the best and avoid the rest.

8. *Compensation That Pays* motivates your people by paying them as co-owners while demonstrating company values through your actions.

9. *Listen More* involves regular interaction with employees to learn from them, show appreciation and document behavior to support promotions or dismissals.

10. *Goals That Work* is a proven method for setting clear goals and following-up consistently to achieve maximum success.

Notice how talking regularly with your team produces results, particularly as you extend those conversations into regular follow-up on goals? This interaction also is critical for you to retain your best people so always make certain it is a priority.

Listen More

Goals That Work

Goals That Work is a proven method for setting clear goals and following-up consistently to achieve maximum success. Here is a quick summary.

✓ Help employees write the first draft of their goals in the TARGET format. (Starting on the bottom of page 157.)

✓ Meet with each employee to write the final draft of each goal together.

✓ Weigh goals to emphasize their importance.

✓ Write goals in two parts: <u>Goal Measurement</u> as a TARGET goal that clearly defines the accomplishment desired, and <u>Goal Description</u> to provide details of how to achieve the goal or what results qualify as exceeding job expectations or outstanding performance.

✓ Document employee progress towards completing goals (Goal Progress Notes).

✓ Follow the 4-step checklist that starts on page 161.

✓ Leverage software to save time writing clear goals in a consistent manner, documenting progress, reminding yourself to follow-up on goals, and confirm completion quickly and easily. Visit our web site for our most current recommendation.

Halftime Reviews

If you hate doing performance reviews, then your employees probably hate receiving them too. However, *employees want to know how they are doing and how to improve.*

Some companies have performance review forms with check-off boxes rating the employee on different behaviors, such as attendance, customer service, and teamwork. These types of reviews have very limited value.

The good news is you can write a comprehensive, custom performance review in 15-30 minutes using software.

But before we jump into how to make performance reviews enjoyable, beneficial and easy, please ask yourself what you are trying to accomplish with the review.

My recommendation is the *Halftime Review* is an important opportunity to confirm your employees are engaged, performing, developing, and most of all, valued assets of your organization. Business is about relationships and performance reviews are a crucial milestone in your journey with each employee.

A *Halftime Review* is similar to how you act as the head coach at a halftime meeting with a sports team during a game. At halftime you discuss the past performance against the desired behaviors and goals set prior to the review period. You then discuss the upcoming review period, including the desired behaviors and goals. Then you instruct and summarize so your team members are clear on your objectives and motivated to perform.

Another reason reviews are important is they can be key documents in the event of an employee lawsuit. Therefore your reviews need to:

- ❏ Be written in a consistent format for all employees

- ❏ Detail employee performance in relation to competencies and goals

- ❏ Include your comments on the individual's performance

- ❏ Confirm the specific timeframe the review is covering

- ❏ Be signed by the employee and yourself

Not including this data makes it difficult to recall those details several years later when you need facts to support a promotion, termination, or defend your company in a lawsuit.

Well-written reviews as part of a consistent year-round performance management system discourage plaintiff attorneys working on a contingency basis. These attorneys only get paid when they win or settle a lawsuit. The better your documentation is written, the less incentive for them to take and file a case.[77]

Using my methods and software, you can invest 15-30 minutes to write a performance review yet it can be 7 pages long. Your reviews are not worded the same for every employee. You can write reviews manually if you prefer. The software just saves you a lot of time.

You can write reviews in three primary ways:

1. <u>Single Rater, Total Control</u>: The review process is confidential. The manager writes the final draft of the review with or without the input of a supervisor, then delivers it to the employee.

2. <u>Single Rater, Shared Control</u>: The manager and employee write the review together, which may take a variety of forms:

   - The employee is asked to submit a self-review, which is reviewed by the manager prior to writing the final review.

- The manager writes a draft review and provides it to the employee for consideration at least 48 hours in advance of their review meeting. They meet to discuss the review in depth and agree upon a final version for signature.

- The manager and employee meet and write the review together.

3. Multi-Rater or 360 Degree:

- A multi-rater review occurs when the manager asks for feedback on the employee's performance from others in the company, including or not including the employee. Then the manager incorporates that feedback anonymously or not anonymously into the final review and meets with the employee to discuss the document.

- A 360 degree review is more subjective in that it is a collection of anonymous feedback from peers, managers and/or executives of the company.

Choose the method that makes you most comfortable. Writing the review from scratch with the employee requires you to be a strong individual because you cannot allow the employee to manipulate you into a better review than is deserved. You must be comfortable pointing out where improvement is needed as well as complimenting her strengths.

My personal preference is to write a draft, put it aside for a day or two; review it again; email it to the employee for consideration; and then meet with the employee to finalize it. Next, consider the key content of a good performance review to decide how to best write reviews yourself.

On page 179 there is an example of a well-written performance review completed in 25 minutes with software. You can do the same manually without software – it just takes you more time.

Design Your Form(s)

The first thing you have to do is design your performance review form. Include goals and competencies from job descriptions for rating at performance review time.

At the top most people call it a performance review. You may call the document a business plan review or something else if you prefer. Write the company name, employee's name and title, reviewer's name and title, and timeframe the review covers at the top also.

Competencies

The first part of the review typically rates competencies by number 1-5, which is consistent with desired behaviors in the employee's job description. Each numerical rating relates to a description of what the number means, such as "Meets Job Requirements" or "Outstanding."

Some companies prefer a 1-3 rating system, but this can be too limiting. For instance using a 1-3 system allows people's performance to be rated as unsatisfactory, satisfactory or outstanding, however an employee may not meet any of these limited descriptions - an employee might be struggling, but not totally unsatisfactory in her performance.

I recommend your rating system be 1-5 and do not use fractions, such as 3.4 except in calculating an average score for a section. Either the person meets the criteria or not. Here are our rating levels:

> 5 – Outstanding
> 4 – Exceeds job requirements
> 3 – Meets job requirements
> 2 – Needs improvement
> 1 – Unsatisfactory

REMEMBER: Rating someone a 3 means she meets the requirements of the job. Many employees expect ratings of 4 and 5, even though they are only meeting job requirements. You must communicate your standards clearly.

Many people get confused in this area because our education system has 5 grade levels: A, B, C, D, and F. In education a "C" average means minimal performance even though it is equivalent to a "3" rating. Therefore either communicate your 5 rating levels clearly – Outstanding, Good and Poor (or whatever words you want).

It is not required for you to use a numerical rating. You can limit the system to only rating someone by descriptors such as, *Meets Job Requirements*, or whatever the numerical rating would mean. Remember we limited the competencies to no more than 6-10 per job description, so this process is not overwhelming unless you are writing the review manually.

For each competency there are often 4-6 factors describing specific behaviors you want from the employee. This means there can be 40-60 different factors that need your comments. Beyond the number and description, you have an entire narrative to write for each factor.

Doing this manually is quite a chore and takes a long time. If you use the software, all you do is rate a factor 1-5 and the software writes the description and narrative for you.

Some people complain at this point, saying they worry about having identical verbiage on their reviews. They feel it looks like they are just copying from one review to the next. They think their employees do not like that, and if it were the case, they would be right.

This view is mistaken. Here is why: Assume for a moment you rated Dick and Jane identically for each factor of the Teamwork competency, so their narratives, description, and numerical ratings are identical.

That is exactly what you want. In a court of law you want both to be identical. If you say something different about Jane than you do about Dick, there is a potential you're being biased. You might be creating a liability because the comments are viewed as unfair. You certainly are inconsistent.

171

The best way to personalize the narrative is to encourage managers to add specific examples, but leave the software-provided narrative untouched. For instance, assume you rate Communications and it has 5 factors. After the provided narrative, start a new paragraph with, "For instance, …" and then copy a Log Event or feedback, or add a comment to validate your rating.

This approach is logical, specific to the employee, and balanced. Unfortunately you always have to consider the legal liabilities. This way you do not accidentally favor a woman over a man or vice-versa.

It is important and beneficial the format remains consistent from one employee to the next, and narratives are completed in a reasonable amount of time because of the software.

If you do this without software, you have to stare at a blank page and think of what to write. This is time consuming and very challenging to be <u>consistent</u> and <u>fair</u>.

One problem when you write a performance review manually is your wording may create a legal liability. The software has a Language Checker that inspects the writing in the review and identifies wording that might be legally inappropriate.

When you fire someone or he quits, take the time to do a performance review for your records. It is in your best interest since you set the employee up in the software with Log Events and Goals to do a performance review that clearly documents your reasons for termination or why the person is leaving your company. It does not take long and provides valuable documentation if the former employee sues you.

Current Goals

Next on my review form are Current Goals for this review period. You want to assess the employee's performance against *Goals That Work*.

You can rate goals 1-5, and then write a narrative about how the person performed. Using a numerical rating is optional. Software can allow you to view, copy and paste verbiage from your Goal Progress Notes and Log Events to the performance review. This saves you time and viewing these items reminds you of past behavior.

Summary

Next you add a Summary on how the employee has done during this review period based on their competency and goal performance. You can write this manually or start with a suggested paragraph or two from the software. The purpose of the Summary is to give an overall perspective on the employee performance during the review period and motivate them to be an achiever in the future.

It is important to personalize the Summary. The software may provide some direction and suggested text, but it must be unique because *many employees focus most on the Summary*. It should not only validate past behavior, but also provide a positive, motivational message about your confidence in the employee to achieve objectives during the next review period.

The Summary should not be used to say the employee was great BUT you expect more. <u>Keep the "big but" out of it</u>. Say something positive about past performance and then motivational words to get them moving positively towards achievement during the next review period.

Two warnings about the Summary section:

❑ Make certain the Summary consistent with what you have written elsewhere in the review. Keep it brief. Do not minimize problems nor be overly praiseworthy.

❑ Be careful not to make promises of any kind. Avoid topics such as promotion, future employment, or bonuses.

Some reviews are written by multiple managers because employees report to more than one manager. Plus, some companies like reviews to have feedback from co-workers.

Multi-rater or 360

You can certainly allow other employees and/or multiple managers to review an employee or manager's performance in regards to Competencies and Current Goals. This is called multi-rater feedback, or a 360-degree process, because an employee gets comments on their performance from people all around them – co-workers, people in other work groups, other managers, and even customers.

A multi-rater review typically returns the feedback from others with their name on it, whereas a 360 review returns the feedback only with the feedback giver's title (anonymous).

Some organizations have tried a 360 process only to have employees try to affect the careers of others by being overly negative or too complimentary. They switched to multi-rater so the person has to include their name with their comments that go to the manager. This enables the manager or company to hold the commentator accountable. Then depending on company policy, the manager can keep the commentator's name confidential from the employee on the review.

Other organizations say they are convinced the feedback must be anonymous for people to be honest.

The use of multi-rater or 360 reviews depends on your company culture. If everyone is working as a team, they can be helpful. Comments from others should not criticize, but focus on how the employee can develop to better serve customers and be a team player.

If your employees do not have the guts to share their opinions openly, or they use the 360-degree process to sabotage the careers of co-workers or only provide positive comments, then the 360 process is a waste of time and a liability.

One interesting aspect of 360 reviews is most organizations expect the second year's performance ratings to increase. Typically the ratings decrease in the second year. Does that mean it was a waste of time? No. It actually indicates your employees are using it more effectively.

The first time employees use a 360 they often do not fully understand the questions and are hesitant to give to critical feedback. The second year they are more familiar with the process and thus are better at assessing their peers. The other reason is if they rated someone positive yet the person did not develop adequately, the employee is more comfortable giving a lower rating to emphasize the need for growth.

Do not get carried away with multi-rater or 360 reviews. <u>The process can be very time consuming</u>. I suggest you start by doing comprehensive *Halftime Reviews* first, and then in the future consider expanding the process to incorporate wider feedback if needed.

Future Goals

Next, list some specific Future Goals with due dates beyond the current review period so they can be discussed. This is because review time is to achieve three objectives:

- ❑ Validate past behavior
- ❑ Summarize how the person has performed during the review period,
- ❑ Discuss future goals and development plans for the upcoming review period.

Development Plans

Some people add development plans into their *Halftime Review*. This is <u>not</u> my recommendation although it is discussed here. I think a development plan is most effective when written and mentored as part of your employee coaching.

Development Plans are an opportunity for you and the employee to identify behavior that Needs Improvement and/or Areas of Strength where the employee can become stronger.

Many people believe you should identify the strengths of your employees and look for new ways to apply those strengths for greater achievement without addressing their weaknesses.

While it can be more productive to build on someone's strengths than focus heavily on weaknesses, certain weak traits must be addressed. Find a balance in your approach to build upon someone's strengths and help the person improve in areas necessary to succeed in their role.

Choose 1-3 Areas of Strength and 1-3 Areas Needing Improvement. Identify goals with action items under the Goal Description for both. The manager should follow-up regularly.

Ideally your employees should write their draft Development Plans. When the employee chooses the behaviors she wants to develop, then she is more motivated to work on them.

If the employee overlooks an Area Needing Improvement you feel is important, as the manager you have the final say. Just try not to discard everything the employee is recommending. She may know her ability to improve in an area is limited based on past attempts.

If an employee refuses to participate in creating Development Plans, and the review includes references to less than satisfactory performance, complete this section yourself and document the employee's explanation for not participating. Documentation is important because this employee may be headed for termination.

A performance review is a key step in consistently, effectively, efficiently managing your people year-round. *It is not a once a year agony, but rather just part of the process.*

Below is a sample performance review written in software. This same format can be followed manually if you prefer.

Performance Review

Employee Name: **Joe Garbanzo**
Job Title: **Team Leader**
Department: **People Services**
Review Period Start: **07/01/2009**
Review Period End: **12/30/2009**
Last Review: **02/10/2009**
Reviewer: **David Russell**
Reviewer Title: **Team Leader**

Rating Ranges

1.00	to	1.74	Unsatisfactory
1.75	to	2.74	Needs improvement
2.75	to	3.74	Meets job requirements
3.75	to	4.74	Exceeds job requirements
4.75	to	5.00	Outstanding

Current Goals

Identify Incentives for Customers   *3.00*
Due Date: 11/15/2009
Weight: 30%
Category: Increase Sales by 10 Percent
Description: Research potential incentives to increase customer satisfaction. Get samples. Show samples to manager and others for input on whether it's most effective. Narrow choices to 5 samples and get group buy-in on the best choice.

Measurement: To establish an incentive for customers that both increases sales and customer satisfaction by 11/15/09.

Result: Joe did an excellent job of going first-hand to see if the salmon was really fresh and thus would be a good incentive for our customers. Fortunately, his quick thinking enabled him to escape from the bear. This turned out to be an excellent incentive.

177

Complete Microsoft MCSE Training   *4.00*
Due Date: 11/01/2009
Weight: 70%
Description: Sign-up for the course early. Make certain to let others know that you will be out of the office those days so your customers are served. Study any appropriate materials in advance.

Measurement: To complete and pass Microsoft MCSE Windows Server training.

Result: Joe completed the training on time and passed with a 100% score at the top of his class.

Competencies
Section Weight: 50%

Communications   *3.80*
Weight: 10%
Expresses ideas and thoughts verbally   *5*
Expresses ideas and thoughts in written form   *5*
Exhibits good listening and comprehension   *3*
Keeps others adequately informed   *2*
Selects and uses appropriate communication methods   *4*

Joe displays superior verbal skills, communicating clearly, concisely, and in meaningful ways. He demonstrates outstanding written communications skills. When communicating, he is very good at selecting and using the most effective methods. Joe listens and comprehends well. However, unless reminded, he sometimes fails to keep others adequately informed.

Cooperation   *2.83*
Weight: 10%
Establishes and maintains effective relations   *3*
Exhibits tact and consideration   *3*
Displays positive outlook and pleasant manner   *4*
Offers assistance and support to co-workers   *2*
Works cooperatively in group situations   *2*
Works actively to resolve conflicts   *3*

Joe regularly displays a positive outlook and pleasant manner. He usually establishes and maintains good working relationships. He exhibits tact and consideration in his relations with others. Joe takes responsibility to help resolve conflicts. However, it would be preferable if he offered more assistance and support to his co-workers. Further, he is not always successful when working in group situations.

Customer Service   3.20
Weight: 10%

Displays courtesy and sensitivity	3
Manages difficult or emotional customer situations	4
Meets commitments	4
Responds promptly to customer needs	3
Solicits customer feedback to improve service	2

Joe is very skillful at resolving difficult or emotional customer situations. He often goes out of his way to make sure commitments are met. He is courteous and displays sensitivity to customers. Joe responds promptly when servicing customers. However, he infrequently uses customer feedback to improve service.

Dependability   3.67
Weight: 10%

Responds to requests for service and assistance	3
Follows instructions, responds to management direction	3
Takes responsibility for own actions	4
Commits to doing the best job possible	4
Keeps commitments	4
Meets attendance and punctuality guidelines	4

Joe willingly accepts responsibility for his actions and their consequences. He continually strives to do the best job possible and he always fulfills his commitments on schedule. Joe shows dependability by beginning work on time and keeping absences to a minimum. When he receives requests for service and assistance, he typically responds courteously and quickly. Joe carries out instructions correctly and responds appropriately to direction.

Job Knowledge   *4.00*
Weight: 10%

Competent in required job skills and knowledge	4
Exhibits ability to learn and apply new skills	4
Keeps abreast of current developments	4
Requires minimal supervision	4
Displays understanding of how job relates to others	3
Uses resources effectively	5

Joe ingeniously puts the resources and tools available to him to maximum use. He demonstrates a high level of competency in the skills and knowledge required. He learns and applies new skills quickly. Joe does an excellent job of keeping himself updated about current developments in his field and he needs a minimal amount of supervision to fulfill his responsibilities. He displays a good understanding of how his job relates to other jobs.

Judgment   *3.60*
Weight: 10%

Displays willingness to make decisions	4
Exhibits sound and accurate judgment	4
Supports and explains reasoning for decisions	4
Includes appropriate people in decision making process	3
Makes timely decisions	3

Joe confidently makes decisions in all areas of his job. His decisions are on target and reflect his reliable, sound judgment skills. He can clearly explain the reasoning and provide good support for his decisions. In most matters, he includes the appropriate people in the decision making process. His decisions are made in a timely manner.

Problem Solving   *3.40*
Weight: 10%

Identifies problems in a timely manner	3
Gathers and analyzes information skillfully	4
Develops alternative solutions	4
Resolves problems in early stages	2
Works well in group problem solving situations	4

Joe is skilled at gathering and analyzing information from multiple sources. He addresses problem-solving situations by analyzing options and developing several alternative solutions. In group situations, he contributes actively to help solve problems. Joe identifies most problem situations within appropriate time frames. However, he could do more to anticipate and resolve problems before they grow into larger issues.

Quality   *3.60*
Weight: 10%
Demonstrates accuracy and thoroughness   4
Displays commitment to excellence   4
Looks for ways to improve and promote quality   4
Applies feedback to improve performance   3
Monitors own work to ensure quality   3

The work Joe produces is usually highly accurate and thorough. He displays a strong dedication and commitment to excellence. He works hard to improve quality in his own work and promotes quality awareness throughout the organization. Joe applies the feedback he receives to improve his performance and he monitors his work to meet quality standards.

Quantity   *3.80*
Weight: 10%
Meets productivity standards   4
Completes work in timely manner   4
Strives to increase productivity   4
Works quickly   4
Achieves established goals   3

Joe usually produces more work than expected and he often completes his work ahead of schedule. He demonstrates a strong commitment to increasing productivity and he works at a faster pace than normally expected for the position. Joe achieves most of his established goals.

Sales Skills   **_3.40_**
Weight: 10%
Achieves sales goals   3
Overcomes objections with persuasion and persistence 5
Initiates new contacts   3
Maintains customer satisfaction   3
Maintains records and promptly submits information   3

Joe expertly uses persuasion and persistence to overcome most any objection. He usually achieves his sales goals and he meets standards for initiating new contacts. Joe responds promptly to the questions and problems raised by his customers. He maintains complete records and meets deadlines for submitting information.

Summary   **_3.62_**
Meets job requirements

Joe continues to make solid contributions to the organization as a reliable performer. He has achieved his objectives and but been a team player encouraging and assisting others.

Future Goals
Market development
Due Date: 12/31/2010
Weight: 50%
Description: Develop the marketing and sales plan to increase affiliate sales. Be the business driver for the product. Take responsibility for product enhancements.

Measurement: To develop $200K in new revenue by December 31, 2010.

Discussion: Please work with the Vendor and internally to develop and implement a successful program.

Yadayada Advisory Board
Due Date: 10/31/2010
Weight: 20%
Description: Participate on the Yadayada Reseller Advisory Board for techno-whizkids. The objective is to gain insights into new technology and tips from other resellers on profitable services they are offering.

Measurement: Completion of one year on the Board, including consistent attendance at meetings and conference calls

Discussion: Leverage these meetings to gain insights into profitable areas of business others are achieving that might be translated into new opportunities for our company.

Development Plans
Strengths to build on
Job Knowledge: You are doing a super job of learning not only our products and services, but truly understanding how they help improve the lives of our customers. Please continue to be a leader in this area and work with me to obtain the additional resources you need to help others follow your lead and for you to further help us improve in this area.

Areas to work on
Communication: Look for ways to divide tasks among group members in order to accomplish work more efficiently. Make sure that difficult, unpleasant, or monotonous assignments are distributed fairly or rotated. When necessary, help others to increase group productivity.

Cooperation: Look for ways to divide tasks among group members in order to accomplish work more efficiently. Make sure that difficult, unpleasant, or monotonous assignments are distributed fairly or rotated. When necessary, help others to increase group productivity.

Employee Comments

Employee Acknowledgment

I have reviewed this document and discussed the contents with my manager. My signature means that I have been advised of my performance status and does not necessarily imply that I agree with the evaluation.

Employee Signature/Date

Reviewer Comments

Joe, once again, you have had a great review period. It's a joy to work with someone who lives with such a passion for excellence and seeks a balance in all that you do on behalf of our company.

Reviewer Signature/Date

United Parcel Service puts it this way:

We Hold Frequent Evaluations With Our Employees About Their Performance

Reviews of each person's performance enable us to arrive at a mutual understanding about progress toward meeting goals and objectives.

We hold formal evaluations periodically. However, there is no substitute for daily and weekly feedback on each person's performance.

We follow up on the results of all evaluations to ensure the continued development of our people.

For the complete list of _UPS' 37 Principles for Managing People_, visit our web site.[78]

Conclusion – 4 Last Important Thoughts

1. Some managers struggle to write reviews because they are concerned about how each employee will respond to it. Reviews should not be a surprise, but rather a confirmation of behavior as you interact regularly with employees as part of the _Success With People_ system.

2. <u>Consider doing your performance reviews 90 days before any compensation review or change in responsibilities</u>. This gives you an opportunity to affirm positive behavior, and state if the behavior continues then the employee earns the raise and/or a change in responsibilities.   For more on compensation, review *Compensation That Pays* (*Desired Result #8*).

   Reviewing performance at the same time as discussing changes to compensation transfers the focus from performance to compensation.   I do <u>not</u> recommend this. *Performance leads compensation, not the reverse.*

3. If you allow your employees to write their own review first (in the software), make certain to find a balance between giving the employee ownership in the process and still holding the employee accountable to deliver strong performance.

4. Lastly, determine how often to do reviews and then stick to it.   Annually is the tradition, but companies like Trader Joe's review their managers annually and part-time employees every 3 months.[79]   Their reviews are a tool to increase employee-manager interaction.

If you diligently work the other aspects of the *Manage Your Team's Performance* suite (*Listen More, Goals That Work*, and *Coach – Do Not Play*), then an annual review is often adequate.

<u>Establish Your Foundation</u>

1. *Systematic Power* is a commitment to hire, manage, develop and retain talent systematically.

2. *Understand How You Make a Difference* makes working for your company a meaningful experience and fuels employee passion to achieve.

3. *LOI: Live It - Observe It - Improve It* involves your employees with your products to increase their passion for your company and ability to serve clients better.

4. *Sanctuary* combines *Rest, Reflect,* and *Risk* to give you a clearer perspective, renewed energy and inspirational creativity to achieve your best.

Balance Your Workload

5. *Success Plans* help you achieve key goals by balancing personal and professional objectives more effectively.

6. *Pass The Baton on Job Responsibilities* efficiently delegates work to your employees.

7. *Right Person – Right Job* is a complete, proven hiring system to hire the best and avoid the rest.

8. *Compensation That Pays* motivates your people by paying them as co-owners while demonstrating company values through your actions.

Manage Your Team's Performance

9. *Listen More* involves regular interaction with employees to learn from them, show appreciation and document behavior to support promotions or dismissals.

10. *Goals That Work* is a proven method for setting clear goals and following-up consistently to achieve maximum success.

11. *Halftime Reviews* transform performance reviews from a once-a-year agony to a motivational meeting that confirms employee past performance and their next bold moves.

As you can see on the next page, *Managing Your Team's Performance* involves listening, managing expectations, supporting their quest for achievement and validating their work. The only thing that is missing is how you fill the gaps. That is covered in our next *Desired Result: Coach – Do Not Play.*

Listen More

**Halftime
Reviews**

**Goals That
Work**

Halftime Reviews transform performance reviews from a once-a-year agony to a motivational meeting that confirms employee past performance and their next bold moves. Here is a quick summary

✓ Your employees want reviews that help them develop – so do it.

✓ Consider the sample performance review on page 177.

✓ Create your own review forms for groups of employees.

✓ Rate competencies fairly and add examples and/or comments to personalize the narrative.

✓ Use Goal Progress Notes and Log Events to comment on the employee's effort and result to achieve the goal.

✓ Summarize the performance during the review period.

✓ List and discuss goals for the upcoming review period.

✓ Development plans can be discussed simultaneously with the performance review, but the development plan ideally should be a separate document.

✓ Discuss the draft copy of the performance review with the employee before finalizing it to make certain you assessment is correct and complete.

✓ Cut the time it takes to write performance reviews in half using software. Visit our web site for our most current recommendation.

Coach – Do Not Play

Desired Result #12

The final *Desired Result* is *Coach – Do Not Play*. I want to quickly emphasize my primary point in coaching:

The objective of coaching is to teach
your people <u>how to think</u>,
rather than just tell them what to do.

As an organization, *Success With People* offers one-on-one coaching to help business people develop more profitable behaviors. We also have the *Success With People Club* which is a low cost way to be mentored monthly and still have the ability to ask specific questions about managing talent.

Coaching.com, a division of The Ken Blanchard Companies did a study with a client where coaching delivered $2 million or more in profits.[80] The findings about the positive benefit of coaching included:

77%	Improved relationships with their direct reports
53%	Increased productivity
67%	Improved teamwork
61%	Improved job satisfaction
48%	Observed better overall quality

Therefore the benefits of having a contract coach are substantial and often accelerate your career. Nevertheless the purpose of this chapter is to focus on how you coach your employees rather than the benefits of contract coaching from any organization.

When you teach your employees to think better, it increases their skills, motivation to do great work and more fully engages them. Worker engagement drives your company's ability to achieve financial success.

Although you are clearly more experienced than your employees, there are aspects to their jobs that are unique to your business and their position in the company. *To be fully competent in every job at your office would be ridiculous!* Plus, often your employees have some natural talent making them better than you ever might be in certain job responsibilities.

Coach – Do Not Play means if you do your employees' jobs for them, you are not making your people more effective and maximizing profits. *You are playing the game rather than coaching the players.* This lead to failure because there is only so much work you can do before you run out of time each day.

Similar to the way you *Pass The Baton on Job Responsibilities* to your people, you need to agree on what needs to be done and then let your people accomplish the objectives. As they run into obstacles, help them think through how to overcome each challenge by asking great, open-ended questions. Here are four key considerations when you are coaching others:

1. This coaching process starts with you. The first step is to recognize that you often know the solution when your employee approaches. He does not even know the right question to ask, but at least he wants to learn. *The desire to learn is the good news!* But if you instantly give him the solution then he never learns how to get there on his own. This may be great for your ego or satisfy your desire for a quick solution, but it is a losing strategy.

2. The next step is for you to mentally prepare yourself. Your job is to understand specifically what the employee wants to talk about. He is coming to you because there is a real or perceived obstacle. Be silent with an encouraging look and pause to consider his current perceived obstacle. Your objective is to establish in your mind, not verbally, the desired outcome of the conversation.

3. Then you want to fully understand the situation so you can confirm your conclusions. To achieve this you must ask open-ended questions to draw out a list of details of the situation and then possible solutions <u>without</u> offering your opinion. Three quick considerations:

   ❑ It sounds hard, doesn't it? Most of us grew-up with parents and coaches who asked very little questions. *They jumped right to the answers.* When you can restrain the "solution reflex" you become a much more effective coach.

   ❑ Every time you give him the answer you lose because you will have to be there next time to answer again.

   ❑ Do not scare or punish him for wrong answers. If even subconsciously the employee feels threatened then you are interfering with his ability to learn and perform at his best.

4. The result of your coaching conversation should be you and the employee have a more thorough understanding of the situation and a number of options. At this point help him select the best option and identify the steps he must take to be successful.

This is hard work <u>for you</u> because you have to think to ask questions about actions you may do instinctively. You have to choose your words carefully. In the past you might have just immediately offered the answer, but that might be why he is coming to you again with a similar question - *you never taught him how to think!*

If you truly want to train your people to perform in an outstanding manner, then whenever possible you must not get in the way of your employees learning with instructions, advice or suggestions. These responses tell him <u>how to do it</u> rather than teach him <u>how to think</u>. New employees may need you to demonstrate how to do the work, but experienced employees need more of an emphasis on how to think on their own. Otherwise you do the work for them.

Successful coaching occurs when desired change demonstrates itself through behavior.

According to J.C. Penney, the founder of the retail chain in his name, *"The greatest single cause of failure in managers is managers don't delegate well to their employees."*[81]

Another big mistake managers make with employees is not following up. We discussed this in *Goals That Work*. You need to regularly observe and measure the success of the actions taken. Be encouraging and supportive, but also strict on holding to the guidelines and timeframe agreed upon. Help him remove any obstacles to his success. Reprimand in private. Give positive recognition in front of his peers.

In many ways coaching drives the success of your business. There are basically three types of coaching.

❑ Coaching for improvement, which is an ongoing process. This is the primary focus of *Coach - Do Not Play*.

❑ Coaching for positive reinforcement, which is the old *"catch someone doing something right."*

❑ Coaching and training to improve in an area because an employee is below your minimum standards, as defined in their job description or goals you have set together.

All effective coaching requires the manager to pause and reflect on the individual situation before commenting. *Do not just jump in and start barking orders!* Leverage *Sanctuary* to focus on the important objectives rather than something that might seem urgent or be emotional.

The more you work the *Success With People* system, the more your responses will be thoughtful, more focused and better communicated than in the past when you reacted instantly to events.

Here are some final quick tips on coaching before we discuss the importance of training. The following are my *7 Habits of Highly Effective Coaches*.[82]

1. Use *Sanctuary* to identify what the individual is doing well and where she needs to improve. In all situations, compare performance against the standards or objectives set in her job description and/or goals.

2. Meet with her, asking open-ended questions about the status of projects or business relationships to determine if she has the same conclusions you have, or whether you need to consider new information. (Ultimately the employee may need to consider new information too.)

3. Ask her how she thinks she is doing, and what actions should be taken.

4. Ask questions on how to proceed.

5. Agree on a direction.

6. Get a firm commitment on the actions she must take, the actions you must do, and the benefit of these actions.

7. Schedule follow-up time to provide support as needed.

When coaching to overcome poor performance, you must pause and reflect to understand what the employee did and why.

Q: Did your employee understand the standards you had set for her? For instance does she have a well-written, up-to-date job description and did she set goals for herself with your approval?

Q: Did she know how to do what you were requiring of her? For instance did she set the goals and job expectations herself and did you observe her ability to achieve the task?

Q: How much of what was going on, either positive or negative, was actually under her control? Maybe your profits are down due to something other than her work. Possibly she is struggling with problems as a result of poor work by another employee.

If you prepare well enough for your coaching meetings about poor performance then your open-ended questions should provide information to confirm what is under her control. Plus her job description and goals should have been carefully crafted to limit responsibilities to what is under her control.

You can also talk with other managers or do some other checking prior to the meeting to confirm how much is attributable to the employee.

> Q: What about feedback? Did she clearly understand how her performance had been prior to this meeting, good or bad?

> Q: Is the employee motivated to succeed? Are there adequate incentives or consequences in place? Remember you work with a wide variety of personalities, all with their own emotional baggage and prejudices. Your job is to be productive with all of them.

An article in The Harvard Business Review has stated, *"The best way to keep your best people is to know them better than they know themselves – and then to use that information to customize the careers of their dreams.*[83]

One of the key ways you achieve this is through coaching.

Remember to view your role as a steward more than a manager. You do not own your people. You have been given financial and people resources to manage. Your responsibility is to grow these assets.

What do you think will be one of your greatest struggles when you coach? Think back to the *Desired Results* we have discussed in the *Success With People* system.

For many people the greatest struggle is slowing down and taking time for *Sanctuary* to prepare yourself mentally to *Listen More* as you coach. Many people instinctively want to give the answers rather than **let their employees work through the process of discovering answers on their own.**

Structure your conversations with employees to allow them to develop an ability to determine the best answer on their own. When you know the answer and no urgent need exists to instantly respond, remain quiet to let your people discover the solution on their own. (You may hear them offering solutions that you overlooked.) Try to question their suggestions in a non-threatening way so they are comfortable expressing themselves.

Close each coaching conversation by confirming the actions they must take, the actions you must take <u>and</u> the benefits of those actions.[84] This assures the employee that she was heard, makes her feel appreciated and motivates her to achieve the actions agreed upon.

Training Supports Coaching

Remember we talked about how successful Don Shula was as the coach of the Miami Dolphins? He is an excellent example of a successful professional coach, yet he never once ran onto the field to do the work he had assigned a member of his football team!

Yet Coach Shula trained his team some days and coached them on others.[85] Training is different from good coaching. Training involves:

1. Explain the objective

2. Show him how to achieve the objective

3. Observe him doing it *(most managers forget this part)*

4. Praise good work and encourage perfection

5. Consider suggestions for improvement from your employees, customers and co-workers

6. Constantly review and revise your training methods to improve effectiveness

7. Never allow an employee to do anything that has not been first perfected in training

A business coach may also train people, but the training process is quite different from coaching as you can see above.

Try watching great college and professional coaches. During the week they train, instruct, and teach players individually and as a team. During the game they may still be the boss who is calling the plays, but you'll notice they also have a dialog with their players to make certain they are thinking on the field. This is because ultimately the player's ability to think during the game determines the outcome more than anything else.

Before the game, then at halftime - remember *Halftime Reviews* - and at the end of the game the coach helps her players understand how to improve their game. Then the coach follows-up in the days and weeks following to make certain each team member learns the skills she identified to be developed.

Coach – Do Not Play connects everything in the *Success With People* system and strengthens all *Desired Results* with repetition and consistency.

Decades ago managers had to train people carefully to do the best job possible. It was a key component to the manager's ability to be promoted. The manager had to make certain their group would still operate strongly when she moved up through the company.

A lot of business problems today seem to be caused by too many people starting companies who have never been formally trained how to operate a business, and college graduates being given management responsibility too quickly. This was a problem of mine during my younger years. Inexperienced people who have not yet grown through it themselves often underestimate the value of years of management training and business experience.

Being a natural leader does <u>not</u> mean you are automatically a good manager of people.

People take a job in part because they feel wanted, but stay with a company because they feel appreciated. In your training and coaching try to communicate you sincerely value your people as part of your team.

Sometimes managers send their employees to seminars for "knowledge dump" training that throws a bunch of ideas at them. True training provides knowledge, tools to deliver efficiencies, coaching for effectiveness and builds upon a <u>system</u> for achievement. There is an important learning process that needs to be experienced.

Therefore training is important. Cris Challender, Director of Training and Organizational Development for WMS Gaming, puts it this way: *"Training is not about creating courses, organizing training events, or spending a training budget. Our mission is to help give people the skills they need to achieve business goals. Training is a **Process**, not an event."*

It is VERY IMPORTANT to train your people only skills and knowledge that you as a manager plan to coach in the weeks, months and years following the training. This type of training has the highest value. <u>Training without follow-up and implementation is usually a waste of time and money</u>.

Another big reason training dollars could be better invested is because some managers do not support the training. Managers intentionally or unintentionally prevent employees from using what they have learned.

For instance, a CEO may mandate others to get training, but does not attend the training herself. Then she continues to do business in a manner that is not incorporating the knowledge or skills learned by her employees in the seminar. If the boss fails to display the desired behavior, then why should the employees?

This type of behavior violates *LOI* and the values statement portion of *Understand How You Make a Difference.*

This is why your training must be supported by a solid system of executive involvement and follow-up to make certain the new knowledge and/or skills are being developed and used regularly.

In a recent study the overall profitability per employee of companies investing highly in workforce learning was 70 percent higher than comparison companies with little or no training. The impact is enormous, however, training on its own is not life changing. It is only one piece of the *Systematic Power* puzzle.

197

Whether you serve as the CEO, manager or employee, you need to be a passionate evangelist behind the improved actions or processes the company is putting in place based on any training.[86]

Get the idea, knowledge, or process embedded into your company's way of managing itself. Then coach people through the process, forcing them to discuss and monitor the key initiatives in at least one management meeting a month.

You may have a situation where an employee was given a task that he should understand how to perform effectively based on his experience before joining your company. You explained the task to him. The employee said he would do it, yet he failed to do it right. You explained to him again what you wanted done. Once again, the employee agreed, but failed to perform correctly.

You may find the problem lies in the fact you have not properly trained the employee. Simply explaining the task in general terms is often not enough. Train the employee to make certain he <u>demonstrates the ability to complete the task</u> at the conclusion of the training. Then coach him as he uses this new skill on the job.

Training in this manner forces you to thoroughly think through the process of completing the task and defining a system for achieving it. You can check with others who are doing similar tasks and incorporate their knowledge into your system. The combination of reflecting on the process, writing it down, gaining the additional expertise of others, training someone and then coaching him needs to be repeated often to constantly evolve best practices.

A recent article quoted a study that training combined with coaching produces an 88 percent increase in productivity.[87]

Back to Coaching

Being effective as a manager comes down to two disciplines:

- ❏ Effectiveness - Managing people and priorities effectively

- ❏ Execution - getting the important things done to grow bottom line performance

Now connect coaching back to profits. To focus your people on company profitability when you coach them, start by establishing realistic expectations about what is to be accomplished at the beginning of any conversation.

The long term benefit and motivation for any objective is the return on investment it provides your company. Coaching people successfully is <u>not about you</u>. Protecting your job is a 'me-focus' whereas developing your co-workers is the "steward-focus" we discussed earlier. *It sustains your company long-term.*

Remember consistent coaching is supposed to be a positive experience for your employee. <u>Be a coach not a critic</u>. Ideally you are listening and asking questions more than telling your employee what to do. *Make your people think!*

When someone on your team makes a mistake, meet one-on-one with him. Start the discussion with an overview of the situation, then offer, *"Maybe I didn't explain this well enough."* Then listen and coach the person to improved performance.

Always avoid a reprimand. Remember you are striving for perfection, but <u>expecting mistakes</u>. Only reprimand when the person has demonstrated the ability to perform yet and fails to execute.

The worst thing you can do when someone is not performing well or makes a mistake is nothing. No response validates the employee's poor behavior. No response is equally bad when someone performs well. It is important to praise and recognize good work to stimulate additional improved performance. Some of this recognition involves rewards and incentives as we discussed in *Compensation That Pays*.

Development Plans

Coaching is ideal to help employees design and complete career development plans. It is in your best interests to create and sustain a system that guarantees the development of leaders throughout your organization for today and the future. Make certain your young leaders are interacting regularly with mentors and learning how to be strategically driven by company goals.

Identifying and developing your next generation of leaders is important for key employee retention. It is often called succession planning because it involves thinking about who will do your job or run your company after you move onto something else.

Succession planning involves identifying the people who you believe may be capable of moving into key positions and then developing a plan to train and test each person for his/her target position. The process involves a lot of coaching.

Coaching is also critical when an employee is allowed to identify a position in your company that she wants to move into at some time in the future. This is often called choosing a career path. It is very motivating to allow your employees to consider a variety of career paths, understand what skills they would need to develop and job experience to complete to qualify for the position.

There are entire books on career pathing and succession planning. For now, I recommend you focus on developing your coaching skills because coaching is critical to both these activities. One book I really enjoyed on coaching was, *Effective Coaching, Lessons From the Coach's Coach by Myles Downey*.

One last thought before we conclude:

No team ever won a major championship without a coach.

We have talked a lot about how you should coach, however, think about yourself for a moment. Where do you want to be in your career in 5 years? If you want to maximize your earnings potential then get a great mentor internally at your company or hire a qualified experienced executive coach even if you have to pay for her/him yourself.

An experienced coach often helps you achieve goals that you cannot accomplish on your own. For this reason many companies pay the costs for managers to have a coach. *Success With People* offers coaching by proven professionals because it works.

Please note that executive coaching is not a substitute for therapy. People often go to therapy for answers to personal struggles. Business people rely on a coach to discover questions that <u>help themselves find better answers</u> for work-related challenges.

Like anything in life, there are good coaches and ineffective ones. Be prepared to pay a reasonable amount for a good coach. Avoid hiring a coach because she is the cheapest. Find someone who is qualified and experienced. Fast Company Magazine recently warned, *"As the price scale (for coaches) slides downward, though, the buyer should beware."*[88]

Conclusion

The way you coach your team is possibly the most important *Desired Result* of the *Manage Your Team's Performance* suite because it gives you regular, focused interaction with your people.

Congratulations! You have learned the entire *Success With People* system. For a quick review you can read individual chapters or the summaries at the end of each chapter.

Check out the final chapter – *The Miracle*. Thank you for investigating *Success With People*! Take a moment now to visit our web site <u>www.SuccessWithPeople.com</u> to sign-up for our free newsletter and learn more about the *Success With People Club*.

<u>Establish Your Foundation</u>

1. *Systematic Power* is a commitment to hire, manage, develop and retain talent systematically.

2. *Understand How You Make a Difference* makes working for your company a meaningful experience and fuels employee passion to achieve.

3. *LOI: Live It - Observe It - Improve It* involves your employees with your products to increase their passion for your company and ability to serve clients better.

4. *Sanctuary* combines *Rest, Reflect,* and *Risk* to give you a clearer perspective, renewed energy and inspirational creativity to achieve your best.

<u>Balance Your Workload</u>

5. *Success Plans* help you achieve key goals by balancing personal and professional objectives more effectively.

6. *Pass The Baton on Job Responsibilities* efficiently delegates work to your employees.

7. *Right Person – Right Job* is a complete, proven hiring system to hire the best and avoid the rest.

8. *Compensation That Pays* motivates your people by paying them as co-owners while demonstrating company values through your actions.

<u>Manage Your Team's Performance</u>

9. *Listen More* involves regular interaction with employees to learn from them, show appreciation and document behavior to support promotions or dismissals.

10. *Goals That Work* is a proven method for setting clear goals and following-up consistently to achieve maximum success.

11. *Halftime Reviews* transform performance reviews from a once-a-year agony to a motivational meeting that confirms employee past performance and their next bold moves.

12. *Coach – Do Not Play* is teaching your people to think on their own so they become better at their work than you.

This is the system of how the *Manage Your Team's Performance* so they achieve mutually agreed upon objectives. It involves listening – *how often do you forget to do that?* – then not just setting goals, but following-up on them; affirming performance and coaching your team to greatness.

If this wheel or motion stops, your team's performance drops also. We like to use software to manage this process so we are more consistent and save time. You can do it any way you like – *just keep it moving!*

**Coach – Do
Not Play**

Listen More

**Halftime
Reviews**

**Goals That
Work**

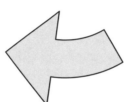

Coach – Do Not Play is teaching your people to think on their own so they become better at their work than you. Here is a quick summary.

✓ Teach your people how to think – do not think for them.

✓ Do not do the work of your employees.

✓ Follow the 7 Steps of Highly Effective Coaches on page 193.

✓ Be an effective trainer by following the 7 steps of training on page 195, but realize the process for training is different than coaching.

✓ Help your people write development plans and give them the support they need to achieve them.

✓ Plan for succession so you have people prepared to step into new roles when people leave.

✓ Get coached yourself to help you achieve more through the _Success With People_ system;

✓ _Success With People_ offers a variety of executive coaching packages to meet your individual needs and budget. Learn more on our web site.

The Miracle

Decades ago I met with a young woman and discussed a major decision in her life. At one point she countered my suggestion with, *"At least I know the right thing to do. Doesn't that count for anything?"*

"No," I replied, *"unless you do the right thing."*

She went on to repeat the major mistake we were discussing several more times in her life.

<u>Do not just read this book and do nothing</u>. Put the *Success With People* system to work for you, your company, employees and customers.

If you are willing to admit you are making mistakes in the way you hire, manage, develop and retain people, then why do you expect your career to improve if you continue to behave the same way?

Why not improve the way you manage talent by implementing a foundational system – *Success With People* – and then build upon it for a truly significant career?

Just as you can cook great food in a variety of ways there are many ways to manage people effectively. The *Success With People* <u>system</u> is my special recipe combining a number of proven actions to bring about the best from your employees. Establish each *Desired Result* and then build upon it with additional knowledge, developed skills, and planned actions.

Spend your days <u>managing -</u> not doing - work your people should be accomplishing.

Have the discipline to use the system and check your activities against it regularly. Systematically move from task to task with *Sanctuary* breaks rather than stressfully racing from activity to activity. Focus on leveraging the system for success each day.

Wrap the *Success With People* system around the value you bring to customers to accelerate your achievements to even greater success.

Ken Thoreson of Acumen Management says, *"Management is the skill of attaining predefined objectives with and through the voluntary cooperation and effort of other people."*[89]

Be prepared for obstacles. Your sincerity, passion and perseverance will enable you to transform your team and/or company. Embark on this as your crusade because managing others effectively is the only way to achieve your goals long-term.

Take the time to make decisions carefully. Leverage *Sanctuary* and the way you *Listen More* to discover how to balance your direction between extremes. Be confident and patient when the process takes longer than planned, yet prepare backup plans in case new information determines a change in direction.

As a manager, you are responsible for financial resources and your company's greatest asset: its people. You're a <u>steward</u> of these assets. A steward is someone who manages property, people and resources that <u>belong to someone else</u>. The good steward protects and adds value to the assets placed under her control.[90]

Properly understood, stewardship is far more significant than a mere word or just another good idea. Understanding your role as a steward is essential to enjoying enduring *Success With People*.

Most managers did not become managers primarily because they wanted to supervise others. They chose the job for more pay, control, or some other reason and then discovered that managing people is really tough.

I encourage you to view managing others as a wonderful gift rather than the burden it is often perceived to be. Find a balance between seeking perfection for yourself and your people, yet expecting imperfection. Do not be shocked by mistakes for they are opportunities for growth. The *Success With People* system is designed to help you avoid mistakes, overcome obstacles, and grow through the unavoidable challenges to become a more effective (and fulfilled) manager.

One book I enjoyed recently is titled, *How to Change The World – Social Entrepreneurs And The Power of New Ideas.*[91] In the book is a story about a social entrepreneur named Fabio Rosa in Brazil who has a dream to provide solar energy to the poorest people throughout his country. He is very fulfilled in life because he spends his days <u>working to achieve something greater than himself</u>.

Rosa once said, *"When we use our intelligence and knowledge to serve people, humanity has hope. We're the hope, we're the future."*

I am honored you have decided to consider the *Success With People* system and put it to good use. It is my sincere hope this system or some lesson in this book helps you develop hope in others and play a significant, positive part in their lives by managing them effectively.

Many people have said it, but I sincerely believe our opportunity to make a difference in this world has never been greater. For all our wonderful technological advances, too many people are unloved, unfulfilled, and have lost hope.

If you are a person of faith then you will spend more time interacting with people <u>at work</u> than during any other activity in your life. How will the way you manage others communicate your faith?

If you are a woman competing in business, do not let others distract you - your greatest opportunities <u>depend on your ability to get things done</u>. Do you have a systematic approach to managing others so you to distinguish yourself as an effective leader?

If you have worked hard to overcome a challenging economic situation, limited education or other obstacles, you must <u>extend your passion to succeed to others</u>. *It is not enough to have passion or even be a natural leader.* Do you have a proven method to lead others to achieve your goals and help <u>them</u> live their dreams?

Many have proven the *Desired Results* of the *Success With People* system work. Now you can leverage what others have learned through great sacrifice to achieve your dreams.

Your employees have all kinds of personal challenges at home. They come to work for a paycheck, <u>but more importantly to add meaning to their lives</u>. Use this system to give them respect, encouragement, and a proven method to accomplish meaningful work.

Conclusion

You spend more time at work than any other single activity. How do you want to be remembered?

I encourage you to **Be Remembered as Someone Who Made a Positive Difference**. The *Success With People* system is designed to help you achieve this goal.

Anyone who helps others to a more fulfilling life by effectively managing them is a miracle worker because supervising others is a tough job. *Be the miracle.*

Let me know how it goes for you. Contact me through our web site - <u>www.SuccessWithPeople.com</u>.

Sincerely,

Appendix

Quotes and Research That Provided Inspiration

[1] Client survey by an associate consulting firm with a top tier automobile parts manufacturer, May 2004. (Client name must remain confidential.)

[2] Council on Education in Management http://www.counciloned.com/onsite/totm-nov2003.asp confirmed 8/19/04 and Automotive Risk Management Insurance Services, http://www.armonline.com/epli.html viewed July 17, 2004.

[3] HR Powerhouse reprinted with permission from CCH, Inc. – http://www.hrpowerhouse.com/Features_1407/workplace_law.asp - confirmed 8/19/04.

[4] Geiger Says Small business Needs Relief From Frivolous Lawsuits, Small-Business Liability Reform, NFIB, 9/29/99 http://www.nfib.com/object/io_1055.html

[5] Dr. Pierre Mornell, as quoted in *Nations Business* as reported by Profiles International in their sales literature.

[6] iLogos Research, a division of taleo (confirmed on August 19, 2004) - http://www.ilogos.com/en/expertviews/articles/strategic/20031007_YL.html.

[7] Tracking Talent for Competitive Advantage, Bill Erickson, Workforce Performance Solutions, April 2005, page 51.

[8] Interview – James Clifton, CEO, Gallup, Inc., www.HR.com, David Creelman, November 25, 2002. http://www.hr.com/hrcom/index.cfm/WeeklyMag/F0F9F4A1-4065-4180-B35A2C8D98C2BCD5

[9] USA Today, September 9, 2004.

[10] Theodore Rex, by Edmund Morris, Random House, New York 2001.

[11] John Adams, by David McCullough, Simon & Schuster, September 3, 2002.

[12] Execution: The Discipline of Getting Things Done, Larry Bossidy and Ram Charan, Crown Business 2002.

[13] Good To Great: Why Some Companies Make The Leap... And Others Don't, Jim Collins, Harper Business 2001.

[14] When Office Love Goes Bad, Sheila Anne Feeney, Workforce.com, February 10, 2004.

[15] Here's A Chicken-And-Egg Conundrum That Could Benefit Us All in The Long Run, Robert Faletra, Computer Reseller News, February 16, 2004.

[16] Harvard Business Review, December 2003, Nike.

[17] Union Blues, What Disorganized Labor Wants, upFront, BusinessWeek, page 12, March 28, 2005.

[18] Creating the Living Brand, Neeli Bendapudi and Venkat Bendapudi, Harvard Business Review, May 2005, page 124. www.harvardbusinessreview.com

[19]   http://www.aboutschwab.com/sstory/missionvision.html - viewed February 17, 2004.

[20] http://www.chevrontexaco.com/about/chevtex_way/vision.asp - viewed February 17, 2004.

[21] http://www.scouting.org/legal/mission.html - viewed June 4, 2004.

[22] http://www.microsoft.com/mscorp/mission - viewed February 17, 2004.

[23] http://www.kenblanchard.com/meetcomp/ourvision.cfm - viewed June 4, 2004.

[24] The Dream Giver Coach Network, Breakthrough Coaching, Presenting Yourself as a Coach, www.thedreamgivercoachnetwork.com.

[25] The Stat, upFront, BusinessWeek, page 14, March 28, 2005.

[26] Interview – James Clifton, CEO, Gallup, Inc., www.HR.com, David Creelman, November 25, 2002. http://www.hr.com/hrcom/index.cfm/WeeklyMag/F0F9F4A1-4065-4180-B35A2C8D98C2BCD5

[27] Living Our Values, Starbucks commitment to social responsibility, ©2004 Starbucks Coffee Company SKU #187462.

[28]
http://www1.us.dell.com/content/topics/global.aspx/corp/soulofdell/en/in dex ?c=us&l=en&s=corp - viewed February 17, 2004

[29] http://corporate.servicemaster.com/overview_objectives.asp - viewed February 17, 2004

30   http://www.ge.com/en/company/companyinfo/at_a_glance/ge_values.
     htm - viewed May 20, 2005

31   In Search of Courage, John McCain, Fast Company Magazine,
     September 2004, page 55.

32   Workers Unhappy In Record Numbers; NYU Career Survey Finds
     They Want Fulfillment More Than Money, Business Wire,
     September 30, 2004.

33   Zig Ziglar, Sell Your Way to the Top, Nightingale-Conant 2002.

34   The CEO Next Door, Ryan Underwood, Fast Company magazine,
     page 64, September 2005.

35   The CEO Next Door, Ryan Underwood, Fast Company magazine,
     page 66, September 2005.

36   Nike corporate slogan in the 1990's.

37   The Power of Full Engagement – Managing Energy, Not Time, Is
     the Key to High Performance and Personal Renewal, Jim Loehr and
     Tony Schwartz, page 172.

38   McKenzie Funk, Popular Science, February 2004, page 59 – "Duke
     University neurobiologist Larry Katz suggests getting up from your
     desk every hour for a change of scenery, even if it's just a trip to the
     water cooler. Unfamiliar sensory stimulation can increase the
     production of brain chemicals calls neurotrophins, he says. In a
     1996 study, Duke University researchers found that neurontrophins
     increase the size and complexity of dentrites – the tendrils on a
     neuron that receive and process information."

39   The Power of Full Engagement – Managing Energy, Not Time, Is
     the Key to High Performance and Personal Renewal, Jim Loehr and
     Tony Schwartz, Free Press.

40   Heart Smart Habit, Medical Update, Reader's Digest, page 49,
     November 2004.

41   If I had my life to live over again, Tony Campolo (out of print –
     Tony has lots of great material. I listed a few in Dave's Book Club,
     or check your local/online book store.)

42   Employee Benefits as a Management Tool, F. John Reh, Your
     Guide to Management,
     http://management.about.com/cs/people/a/Benefits100198_p.htm

43   How to Live an Unbalanced Life, Keith H. Hammonds, Deputy
     Editor, Fast Company, page 70, October 2004.

[44] Top 10 Leadership Tips from Jeff Immelt, Fast Company, page 96, April 2004.

[45] Council on Education in Management http://www.counciloned.com/onsite/totm-nov2003.asp confirmed 8/19/04 and Automotive Risk Management Insurance Services, http://www.armonline.com/epli.html viewed July 17, 2004.

[46] Descriptions Now software from Adminstaff.

[47] Client survey by an associate consulting firm with a top tier automobile parts manufacturer, May 2004. (Client name must remain confidential.)

[48] Steve Tessler, Senior Partner, CheckPoint HR, www.checkpointhr.com

[49] Tracking Talent for Competitive Advantage, Bill Erickson, Workforce Performance Solutions, page 48, April 2005.

[50] Job Patterns Must Change, If Your Business Has Changed! Case Study, Employer's Advantage newsletter, Profiles International, April 20, 2004.

[51] Aegis Lending Documents Improvements, Employer's Advantage newsletter, Profiles International, March 26, 2004.

[52] Job Fit or Mis-Fit? Performance Based Dismissals, Jay Werth, CareerLife Resources, Employer's Advantage, Profiles International, February 25, 2004.

[53] Shandel Slaten, True Life Coaching, www.truelifecoaching.com.

[54] Example provided by Shandel Slaten, True Life Coaching, www.truelifecoaching.com, March 26, 2004.

[55] More Missed Background Checks, Workforce Week, August 15-21, 2004, Vol. 5, Issue 30, www.workforce.com.

[56] Teams built to last, Barry Wilner, Associated Press, published in the Marin Independent Journal, February 6, 2005.

[57] Many Companies Don't Do Enough To Benefit From Performance-Based Pay Plans, Peek Performance, February 2004 – Vol.1, Issue 12, Page 2, Business Wire, May 5, 2004.

[58] Many Companies Don't Do Enough To Benefit From Performance-Based Pay Plans, Hewitt Associates press release, Peek Performance, www.synygy.com/peekperformance.Vol1Issue15p002.html, May 5, 2004.

[59] Working and Poor, Michelle Conlin and Aaron Bernstein, Business Week, McGraw-Hill Publishing, page 61, May 31, 2004.

[60] Nucor Fastener Division, The Nucor Story, www.nucor-fasterner.com/nucor.html viewed June 3, 2004.

[61] Managing Google's Idea Factory – Marissa Mayer helps the search giant out-think its rivals, BusinessWeek, October 3, 2005, page 88.

[62] Beyond Manipulating and Motivating to Leading and Inspiring, Jim Clemmer, HR.com, quoting Jeffrey Pfeffer, "Six Dangerous Myths About Pay," Harvard Business Review.

[63] Human Resources and Company Performance, Naomi Giszpenc, The ESOP Association, The ESOP Report, April 2003, pg. 3. www.esopassociation.org

[64] United Airlines, ESOPs, and Employee Ownership, Corey Rosen, ESOP Executive Director, NCEO, November 2002 http://www.nceo.org/library/united_esop.html

[65] In a generation, gap separating compensation of chiefs, others widens, Bruce Murphy, Milwaukee Journal Sentinel, October 9, 2004.

[66] Avoiding Employment Litigation: A Practical Approach, Epstein Becker & Green, P.C., Workforce Management email, November 6, 2003.

[67] How to Give Feedback, page 103, Fast Company, Seth Godin, March 2004.

[68] Matthew 23:11-12, Life Application Study Bible, Tyndale House Publishers and Zondervan Publishing, page 1701.

[69] 65% of Americans receive NO praise or recognition in the workplace, email from www.bucketbook.com (the Gallup Organization), August 18, 2004.

[70] How to Turn Managers Into Leaders, Nathaniel Welch, Business 2.0, page 70, September 2004.

[71] The Five Love Languages – How to Express Heartfelt Commitment to Your Mate, Gary Chapman, Moody Publishers, June 1996.

[72] National Seminars speaker event, January 4, 2005.

[73] High Performance, Cindy Waxer, Human Resource Executive magazine, March 2004.

[74] Living in Dell Time, Bill Breen with Michael Aneiro contributing, Fast Company Magazine, November 2004, page 86.

[75] Use one-on-one sessions to guide your team, Ken Hardin, TechRepublic, January 10, 2002, http://techrepublic.com.com/5100-6314_11-1038833.html

[76] Everyone's a Coach – You Can Inspire Anyone to be a Winner, Ken Blanchard and Don Shula, page 75, Harper Business – Zondervan Publishing House 1995.

[77] To Appraise or Not to Appraise, HR Spotlight, Ned Roberts, SPHR and John Ricco, Esq., HR West Magazine of the Northern California Human Resources Association, Volume 2, Issue 1, 2004.

[78] UPS' 37 Principles for Managing People, Workforce Management magazine, http://www.workforce.com/archive/article/24/03/43_printer.php

[79] Shopper's Special, Irwin Speizer, Workforce Management Magazine, September 2004, pages 51-54 or www.workforce.com.

[80] Coaching Improves Productivity, Madeline Homan and Linda Miller, Coaching.com, www.coaching.com/Marketing/Common/newsproductivity.htm viewed 8/31/04.

[81] Dale Carnegie Weekly Tip email, www.DaleCarnegie.com.

[82] Inspired in part by the book, Everyone's a Coach – You Can Inspire Anyone to be a Winner, Don Shula and Ken Blanchard, Harper Business – Zondervan Publishing House, 1995; Carnegie Success Connection February 23, 2004.

[83] Job Sculpting: The Art of Retaining Your Best People, Harvard Business Review, September-October 1999, submitted to the author of this book by Al Rinaldi.

[84] Million Dollar Consulting, Alan Weiss, McGraw Hill, New York 1999.

[85] In part inspired by Everyone's a Coach – You Can Inspire Anyone to be a Winner, Ken Blanchard and Don Shula, Harper Business – Zondervan Publishing House 1995. I have also seen several of these steps recommended by other authors.

[86] Hidden Asset, Fast Company, Bill Breen, page 94, March 2004.

[87] www.profilesinternational.com, Profiles International web site quoting Workforce Magazine, October 2000.

[88] Are You Being Coached?, Ryan Underwood, Fast Company Magazine, Page 85, February 2005.

[89]   Ken Thoreson, www.acumenmanagement.com, November 10, 2004.

[90]   Stewardship Principles That Make a Difference, Money Matters, Crown Financial Ministries, February-March 2004, page 3.

[91]   How to Change the World – Social Entrepreneurs and the Power of New Ideas, David Bornstein, page 39, Oxford University Press, New York 2004.